ONLINE COMMUNITIES OF PRACTICE:

CURRENT INFORMATION SYSTEMS

RESEARCH

Gregg Greer

DEDICATION

I dedicate this to my wonderful wife who has constantly supported my academic and professional endeavors.

CONTENTS

ACKNOWLEDGMENTS

This book would not be possible without the help of my mentors:

Dr. Amit Deokar
Associate Professor of Information Systems
College of Business and Information Systems
Dakota State University

Dr. Surendra Sarnikar,
Assistant Professor of Information Systems
College of Business and Information Systems
Dakota State University

Dr. Viki Johnson
Associate Professor of Sociology
College of Arts and Sciences
Dakota State University

This book would also not be possible without the patience of my family and the support of my colleagues at Lubbock Christian University.

ABOUT THE AUTHOR

Gregg Greer is an Assistant Professor in the College of Professional Studies at Lubbock Christian University. He has taught courses in Information Systems since 2007.

He is pursuing a doctorate in Information Systems through the online D.Sc. program at Dakota State University and is currently working on his dissertation. He is studying the area of Knowledge Management and Decision Support.

His research interests include online communities of practice, design of online communities, online analytical processing and business continuity planning in higher education.

Part One: Online Communities of Practice

Abstract

This book comprises a preliminary literature review for the topic of online communities of practice. An online community of practice allows community members to share knowledge and social support on a topic of interest through computer-mediated communication. How can organizations develop and maintain online communities of practice? When creating communities of practice, organizations face the challenge of crafting an online environment that encourages broad-based participation by the community it serves. Communities which do not engender knowledge sharing between their members ultimately die. A consulting firm estimated that about half of the on-line communities set up by Fortune 1000 companies will not live up to expectations (Ransbotham et al. 2011). What factors encourage knowledge sharing behaviors and continued participation?

Part one of this book introduces online communities of practice and then examines three types of factors which affect the success of knowledge sharing in online communities of practices: Individual Motivations, Community Factors and Technological factors (Erat et al. 2006). Part two of the book summarizes by theme the journal articles referenced in part one as well as additional articles on similar topics.

Chapter One: Introduction

Online communities of practice enable people from disparate geographical areas to communicate and exchange information on a wide variety of subjects. Many organizations use online communities of practice to facilitate knowledge sharing (Ardichvili et al. 2003). Many independent communities of practice cross organizational boundaries. Unfortunately, having access to an online community of practice often does not encourage community members to participate in knowledge sharing activities that benefit the entire community. Group members may not wish to or cannot easily share their knowledge with other group members (Ardichvili et al. 2003).

Typically, online communities are volunteer efforts, with the rewards for participation existing only in the context of the online community (Bateman et al. 2011). Unfortunately, poorly designed or poorly run sites loose membership and become stagnant or perish completely. Technical issues cause these problems in some cases, but often a failure to create effective collaborative processes in its members results in a high turnover rate (Ransbotham et al. 2011). Many visitors to online communities do not return after their initial visit. However, some visitors do return and engage in the behaviors which make the community work: reading posts, writing posts and moderating the group (Bateman et al. 2011). Successful communities of practice are able to draw out participation from community members. Knowing what motivates members to participate within the community allows the community stakeholders to create effective communities of practice.

This e-book is a direct result of a review of academic research during the pursuit of a doctoral dissertation. In order to better understand communities of practice, a number of terms will be defined. The differences between face-to-face and online communities of practice will be enumerated. The research problem will be stated as well as the relative importance of research on communities of practice. Some theories are listed which have been used to explain the dynamics of online communities.

Definition of Terms

Preece defines online communities as groups communicating in a virtual space for a specific reason, with supporting technology and rules of behavior (Trier 2008). One of the goals of an online community of practice is to share knowledge. The literature discusses the following types of communities of practice: professional virtual communities, private customer communities, customer cross-border communities, business customer communities, and Electronic Networks of Practice.

Knowledge Sharing

Knowledge sharing occurs when people communicate explicit or tacit knowledge from one person to another. People write down or codify explicit knowledge. Tacit knowledge only exists in the minds of the people who know it. Some researchers argue that while people can share explicit knowledge using technological means through the organization's structure, they can only communicate tacit knowledge interpersonally (Chang et al. 2010). People can act on knowledge which is shared effectively. Knowledge sharing can take place between individuals, within organizations or across organizations (Becerra-Fernandez et al. 2004).

Community of Practice

Lave and Wegner define a community of practice as "an activity system about which participants share understandings concerning what they are doing and what it means in their lives and for their community" (Erat et al. 2006). Lave and Wegner also defined a community of practice as "a group of people who share an interest in a domain of human endeavor and engage in a process of collective learning that creates bonds between them" (Gray 2004). In an online community of practice, computer technology mediates the primary relationships between the members. Wegner defines four main characteristics of a community of practice. Practice explains that the community centers around the practical application of knowledge through the successful completion of tasks. Community describes the social learning that takes place as members with a basic level of knowledge collaborate. Experience indicates that members share their experiences within the group, generating relevant and applicable knowledge. Finally, Identity indicates that the member incorporates the community of practice and the member's role within it into the member's self-concept (Hara et al. 2007). Communities of practice differ from other types of communities in the following ways. Typically, members organize the community of practice, they focus on a specific area of interest and the community expects group members to have some level of competence in that area, the group members interact and form relationships, and they create a shared body of knowledge shared by the entire group (Gray 2004). Communities of practice typically go through the following phases in their life cycle: Preparing, Planning, Initiating, and Sustaining (Erat et al. 2006). Communities of practice typically help members to do the following: learn details about their job performance, place their work in a meaningful context, visualize the organization, refine their professional self-image, share technical and informal social skills, become "enculturated" into the community, move between the core and fringes of the group (Gray 2004).

Professional Virtual Communities

Business professionals form Professional Virtual communities that regularly communicate through online media such as a bulletin boards or newsgroups. Virtual Professional communities face the difficulty of ensuring a continual supply of new knowledge from members (Chen et al. 2010).

Private Customer Communities

Customers for a particular vendor form private customer communities and meet in a secured on-line setting typically maintained by the vendor.

Customer Cross-border communities

A vendor's employees and customers form customer cross-border communities to develop new ideas for products and processes.

Business Customer Communities

Customers of a particular vendor create business customer communities and transfer and share knowledge in order to help improve each other's performance. Customers may create a business customer community as a grassroots effort that does not necessarily need the support of the vendor, which makes it differences private customer communities and cross-border business communities.

Electronic Networks of Practice

An electronic network of practice shares knowledge and collaborates over computer-mediated technology. Electronic networks of practice cross organizational and national boundaries. A common interest draws members together. Wikipedia.org is a good example of a network of practice. (Wasko et al. 2009)

Differences between Face-to-face and Online Communities of Practice

Agarwal, Gupta and Kraut (2008) list three differences between online social networks and real-world social networks: scale, communication dynamics, and user-generated content. Geography and time zones do not limit the scale of on-line social networks. However, on-line communities do have some limitations of scale that differ from real-world social networks. The communication dynamics in an online social network differ from those in a real-world network. For instance, when someone communicates face to face, they can use body language to determine whether or not they should trust someone. Online, users must use different techniques. Online communities also show a difference in the creation of user-generated content. Inexpensive and efficient communication of information makes this possible (Agarwal et al. 2008).

Research Question

What essential success factors influence whether its member adopt an on-line community as evidenced by knowledge sharing behaviors? When does a community become useful enough to elicit long-term participation?

Importance of research

Online communities of practice enable people from disparate geographical areas to communicate and exchange information on a wide variety of subjects. However, communities lose this opportunity when poorly designed or poorly run sites loose membership and become stagnant or perish completely. A consulting firm estimated that about half of the on-line communities set up by Fortune 1000 companies will not live up to expectations. Technical issues cause this in some cases. In other cases, a failure to create effective collaborative processes result in a high turnover rate which decreases the effectiveness of the group (Ransbotham et al. 2011).

Theory Base for research

Online Community theories come from the diverse fields of Management, Sociology, Psychology, Computer Science and Information Systems. The field of management contributes theories about the loyalty of customers, organizational structure, and how organizations store knowledge. Sociology contributes theories about a person's identity, the face-to-face community they live in, "Social Capital" and how people behave in groups. Psychology contributes the factors the make a community, and what drives people to behave in desired ways. Computer Science provides the theories for the technology, specifically the Internet. Information Systems contributes the Life Cycle of computer systems, development of web computer systems, and theories for meeting the members' needs for socialization, easy-to-use software, information security and safety (Iriberri et al. 2009).

Some additional examples of theories used for research into on-line communities include:

- Collective Action (Wasko et al. 2009)

- Communities of practice (Gray 2004; Hara et al. 2007; Silva et al. 2008)

- Contemporary Tribalism (Campbell et al. 2009)

- Economic Stochastic model (Mayer 2009)

- Factors which increase community knowledge (Chen et al. 2010)

- Game Theory (Ba 2001)

- Gift-giving theory (Bergquist et al. 2001)

- Information Processing Theories (Forman et al. 2008)

- Informational Cascades (Duan et al. 2009)

- Kane's collaboration model with two phases: creation and retention. (Ransbotham et al. 2011)

- Knowledge Integration (Robert et al. 2008)`

- Knowledge sharing theories (Chang et al. 2010; Chen et al. 2010)

- Marketing Theories (de Valck et al. 2009)

- Public Goods (Wasko et al. 2009)

- Resource-based theory of sustainable social structures (Butler 2001; Ibrahim et al. 2009)

- Social capital (Chang et al. 2010; Robert et al. 2008)`

- Individual motivation, and participant involvement (Chang et al. 2010)

- Social Disorganization Theory (Wareham et al. 2007)

- Social Exchange theory (Posey et al. 2010)

- Social Network Analysis (Trier 2008; Wasko et al. 2009) SNA performs quantitative analysis on interrelated social patterns between people.

- Social Penetration Theory (Posey et al. 2010)

- Transaction-cost Economics (Ibrahim et al. 2009)

Significant Prior Research

The following summarizes a number of articles which deal with online communities and groups them by theme. Research into online communities of practice reveals the following themes of factors which encourage people to share knowledge in online communities of practice. Qualities of the individual and qualities of the community and qualities of the technological environment encourage members to share knowledge.

Chapter Two: Individual Motivations

Internal qualities and expectations motivate individuals. Many individual factors have been described as influencing behavior in online communities. Social capital is the intrinsic and extrinsic worth of an individual's social network. Trust and the Perception of Reciprocity are two components of social capital that have been studied outside of the context of social capital. The perception of enjoyment and how the member feels they belong with the group also seem to influence behavior in online communities of practice (Lu et al. 2011).

Members participate in an online community and share knowledge when they feel it will build their social capital and make additional resources available to them (Ganley et al. 2009). Perception of reciprocity describes how the individual believes other members of the community will act in sharing knowledge. Individuals that believe other members will reciprocate their efforts to share knowledge will more likely to share knowledge (Chang et al. 2010; Chen et al. 2010). Reciprocity also increases the likelihood the members will self-disclose online (Posey et al. 2010).

The confidence a group member has in their ability to provide usable knowledge to the group describes knowledge sharing self-efficacy. Group members who feel they have more to contribute, tend to contribute more (Chen et al. 2010).

Perceived relative advantage describes how the group member perceives the result of their sharing knowledge. If the group member believes they will get a higher return from sharing knowledge than the investment sharing knowledge takes, then they will be more likely to share knowledge (Chen et al. 2010).

Perceived compatibility describes the "fit" between the shared knowledge and the needs of the community. Group members share knowledge more often when they judge that their knowledge sharing behaviors match the purpose and focus of the group (Chen et al. 2010).

Social capital describes the socioeconomic value of a person's social network. Members participate in an online community and share knowledge when they feel it will build their social capital and make additional resources available to them (Ganley et al. 2009). Chang and Chuang (2010) describe three dimensions of social capital. The structural dimension of social capital describes the extent of the interpersonal linkages between group members and departments within a community. The relational dimension describes the relationship between a group member and the organization itself. "Trust, norms, obligations, expectations and identification" make up the components of the relational dimension of social capital. The common understandings and assumptions shared by a community make up the cognitive dimension. A shared language and codes make up the components of the cognitive dimension (Chang et al. 2010). Structural and cognitive social capital have more importance for virtual teams. On-line or virtual environments require relational capital. (Robert et al.

2008)

In face-to-face communities of practice, members learn to trust each other through a series of interactions. Online communities find building trust more challenging because the members often never see each other and members may infrequently interact online. Online community members share more knowledge when they believe they can rely on the other members of the community to provide honest, accurate information and not misuse information (Chen et al. 2010). Trust also increases the likelihood the members will self-disclose (Posey et al. 2010). In the context of e-commerce, Ba (2001) describes several levels of trust. Deterrent or Calculus-based trust means that someone acts in a trustworthy way because they fear the negative consequences of acting untrustworthily. Information-based trust allows members to predict the actions of the others because of their previous interactions with each other. Transference-based trust allows trust means that if one member trusts another member, the member can trust any third parties trusted by the intermediary (Ba 2001).

Identification occurs when a member sees themselves as part of a community. The image a group member presents to a community reflects their identification with the community. Members who identify themselves as members of the community typically remain active members of the community (Chang et al. 2010). When a community shares a language or codes, they can share knowledge more easily (Chang et al. 2010). Community members share knowledge more when they feel their reputation within the community will increase (Chang et al. 2010). Many members of a community will share knowledge because of their altruism, or the sense they have that their contributions help other people and they feel appropriate behavior requires helping others (Chang et al. 2010; Cheliotis 2009).

Individual rewards can encourage people to contribute their knowledge to the community. Xu, Jones and Shao surveyed Open Source Software developers and found that developers contributed to the community because of the rewards they thought they would receive. Specifically, the developers needed the end product, expected that their reputation and skills would improve and because they enjoyed the work (Xu et al. 2009). Financial incentives can also drive members' motivations to share knowledge (Cheliotis 2009).

Social exchange theory proposes that people will engage in a community only as long as the perceived benefits outweigh the perceived costs (Posey et al. 2010). Posey suggests that the perception of a risk to privacy will decrease members' tendency to self-disclose (Posey et al. 2010). Members from collectivist cultures, self-disclose more than those from cultures with weak social ties (Posey et al. 2010).

In the realm of Open Source Software Development Groups, Hahn, Moon and Zhang suggest that people join communities and share knowledge when they know the group leader and when the developers on the team have strong reputations (Hahn et al. 2008).

Gregg Greer

Social Capital

Social capital is the socioeconomic value of a person's social network. Members participate in an online community and share knowledge when they feel it will build their social capital and make additional resources available to them (Ganley et al. 2009). Social capital can be envisioned as containing three dimensions. The structural dimension of social capital describes the extent of the interpersonal linkages between group members and departments within a community. Ganley and Lampe (2009) examine online communities through the lens of social capital and social networking theory. Robert, Dennis and Ahuja (2008) used the theory of social capital to explain how teams integrated knowledge.

The theories of social capital, individual motivation and participant involvement all play a part in determining why people share knowledge in on-line communities. (Chang et al. 2010) Chang and Chuang use the theories of social capital and individual motivation to describe why people share knowledge within online communities. They innovatively combine the theories of Social Capital and Individual Motivation to more completely describe the knowledge sharing process. Chang and Chuang conducted a survey and found that knowledge sharing is positively influenced by altruism, identification, reciprocity, and shared language. Reputation, social interactions and trust had positive effects on the quality, but not the quantity of shared knowledge. The participant involvement moderates the relationship of altruism and the quantity of knowledge shared. This article had an excellent diagram explaining the interaction of social capital theory and individual motivations. The authors also included the text of the survey they used to measure their constructs. They suggest the following research questions. Do different types of on-line communities behave in different ways? Do "lurkers" in the community fill out voluntary surveys less often than other members and underrepresent themselves in the results? (Chang et al. 2010) Chang and Chuang do not look closely at the community factors which can influence knowledge sharing. So, future research could expand their model to contain other facets as well.

Robert, Dennis and Ahuja (2008) studied team interactions over "lean" digital networks. They conducted an experiment with forty-six teams with prior histories and anticipated future relationships and gave them tasks to perform in person and online. They used the theory of social capital to explain how the teams integrated knowledge. Robert breaks social capital down into structural, cognitive, and relational social capital. They assert that social capital can answer part of the following question: Why do team members not integrate knowledge from other team members? Virtual teams found structural capital and cognitive social capital more important to knowledge integration. Relational capital remained important regardless of the environment. Knowledge integration helped teams make better decisions. Their study had some limitations. They used student subjects and it is difficult to operationalize cognitive capital. (Robert et al. 2008)` Future research might use a similar experimental research method with a different theory. Future research might also compare how teams with and without a history together performed. Experiments could be conducted online first and then face to face and vice versa.

Fang and Neufeld (2009) use the theory of Legitimate Peripheral Participation to explain sustained participation in OSS (Open Source Software) projects. They define situated learning as learning in everyday practice, learning that connects people, actions, knowledge and the surrounding world. Identity construction happens as a group member incorporates their group membership into their self concept and builds their self-esteem somewhat on their approval by the group. The individual motivations that get someone involved in an OSS project do not drive their sustained participation. Situated learning and identity construction most influence sustained participation in an OSS project. Sustained participation also influences situated learning and identity construction. They suggest the following areas for future research. First, future research could empirically test their model. Second, researchers could collect additional primary data by interviewing programmers. Third, researchers could use quantitative surveys to make the results more generalizable. Fourth, research could examine the role of community level factors to the model. Fifth, researchers could examine power and roles to see how they factor into participation. Fourth, future research could examine the role of Bourdier's theory of practice.

Ganley and Lampe (2009) used quantitative analysis of the Slashdot.org community to apply social capital and social networking theory to online communities. How do communities which only offer virtual rewards get people to dedicate real time toward creating content? Ganley and Lampe look at how Individual motivation encourages members to generate high quality content for the website with virtual rewards. People create social networks of direct and indirect relationships because of the resources they offer. The socioeconomic value of a person's network represents their social capital. Social capital enables someone to gain benefit from their interactions with others. Ganley and Lampe (2009) look for "Structural holes". When pathways or bridges of less populated segments surround two densely populated network clusters, the less populated areas may form a structural hole. Brokers reach across structural holes. Brokerage in networks gives more new information from different sources. Closed systems do not connect to other network segments. A closed network may give increased social capital to its primary members. These closely knit groups trust each other more. Closure in networks helps groups maintain focus on specific goals and ideas.

People with broader networks tend to have more structural holes and lower social capital. People with deeper networks have fewer structural holes and more social capital. Ganley and Lampe (2009) propose changes to the mechanisms of online communities that will make them more successful. They also suggest creating a "What my friends are saying" page for brokers and invitation only "power user" forums for people with a high degree of closure.

Ganley and Lampe suggest that future researchers might use more extensive data collection and include information from other communities. They suggest qualitative surveys to topically examine relationships. They ask how basic organizational theory translates into on-line communities (Ganley et al. 2009). Researchers might conduct an experiment giving members the opportunity to participate in communities which fit the following criteria: anonymous, not anonymous, but have no "karma" system in place, or have a system similar to Slashdot's "Karma" in place.

Perception of Reciprocity

Some individuals share knowledge because they expect other members will reciprocate. They expect to gain from other individuals sharing knowledge. Reciprocity describes how the individual believes other members of the community will act in sharing knowledge. Individuals that believe other members will reciprocate their efforts to share knowledge will more likely to share knowledge (Chang et al. 2010; Chen et al. 2010). Reciprocity also increases the likelihood the members will self-disclose online (Posey et al. 2010). Bergquist and Ljungberg (2001) researched open source development communities through the lens of gift giving theories. As seen above, reciprocity is sometimes discussed as a component of social capital and other times discussed as a separate construct. Chen and Hung (2010) show that reciprocity, trust, knowledge sharing self-efficacy, perceived compatibility and perceived relative advantage affect positively affect knowledge sharing. Xu, Jones and Shao (2009) propose that the perception that contributions will be returned in kind, along with a number of other factors, improves knowledge sharing in open source software projects.

Bergquist and Ljungberg (2001) examined open source development communities. They used the theories of gift giving to explain knowledge sharing in a digital domain. The gift economy creates openness and organizes relationships. Open source software communities generate new ideas by giving gifts. The giver receives power by giving and uses it to guarantee code quality. Their research raises the following questions. Their research might validated by applying it to a different type of online community. Users in other types of groups may not gain "power" as such by their contributions. They used a virtual ethnography to study the OSS groups. Another approach might involve an experiment, focus groups, or a survey of groups. Future research might also use social network analysis might as an approach to study the affect of giving a "gift" of knowledge on relationships within the group.

Chen and Hung (2010) use individual motivation theory to explain why people share knowledge in Professional Virtual Communities. Chen and Hung gathered survey data from two virtual communities and used structured equation modeling to verify the factors which influence the increase of community knowledge. Reciprocity, trust, knowledge sharing self-efficacy, perceived compatibility and perceived relative advantage affect knowledge sharing. Knowledge contributing and collecting positively affected knowledge utilization. Knowledge collecting affected community promotion. Knowledge contributing had a limited effect on community promotion. This article has an excellent diagram of an integrated framework for knowledge sharing and the survey questions they used to measure their constructs. They suggest that further studies might include wider data, since their information came from only two communities. They also suggest that a longitudinal study over the life cycle of a community might also reveal additional information. They also wonder how the level of knowledge activity influences the financial Contribution of the PVC (Chen et al. 2010). Additional research questions might include the following. How do inter-organizational Professional Virtual Communities differ from intra-organizational communities of practice? How do Professional Virtual Communities compare to Business Customer Communities where the members can compete with members use the same vendor?

Xu, Jones and Shao (2009) studied open source software projects and the motivation of people who contribute to them. Xu asks why people contribute to Open Source Software projects by creating a research model which includes individual and community factors. They surveyed volunteer OSS developers. Involvement helps determine performance. The following individual motivations drive involvement: personal software needs, expectation of increased skills and reputation, and enjoyment. Project community also plays a part with factors such as: the effectiveness of the leadership, interpersonal relationship, and the ideological basis of the community. The authors suggest that future studies might examine a different OSS environment to test the generalizability of their results. They also suggest that since they only examined active projects, their data underrepresents projects which completed successfully or failed outright (Xu et al. 2009).

Posey, Lowry Roberts and Ellis (2010) researched French and British users and how they disclosed personal information on social networking sites. Even though they do not address knowledge sharing directly, self-disclosure approximates sharing knowledge. The researchers see self-disclosure as relevant because businesses can use such self-disclosure to market to individuals. They used the social exchange theory which says that the benefits of the community must outweigh the costs. Social penetration theory suggests that people self-disclose to build relationships. The authors also theorize that people with stronger tendencies toward collectivism self-disclose more than people from cultures with weaker relational ties. The main benefit of self-disclosure is that the other party may also self-disclose. The main drawback of self disclosure is putting oneself at risk. They used a market research firm to randomly select British and French social networking users, taking special care to stay away from people who are in the normal range for college. They discovered the following relationships. Positive social influence, reciprocity, and trust positively influence self-disclosure. In their study, positive social influence measures the social pressure to use online communities, not actual disclosure. Privacy risk perception decreases disclosure. People from collectivist cultures with stronger ties between individuals self disclose more than non-collectivist cultures. For instance, the French are more individualistic than the British. The authors suggested that future research might include a broader concept of anonymity. Future research might also indicate other factors besides individualism and collectivism. Research might also investigate how communities should reward collectivism? Since the respondents filled out the surveys themselves, the data does not reflect how the respondents' perceptions might differ from reality. The authors also suggested a longitudinal study to better measure social penetration. The original study did not examine additional aspects of Social Penetration Theory such as satisfaction, stability and security. Also they questioned whether or not it is ethical to get people to self-disclose to market to them (Posey et al. 2010). Knowledge sharing might be measured in the same way as self-disclosure in this study. Posey suggests that the perception of privacy risk decreases self-disclosure. In an on-line community, a lack of system security would discourage knowledge sharing. Future research might also find the differences in self-disclosure in online communities and online communities of practice.

Romano, Pick and Roztocki (2010) review literature on collaboration in interorganizational and cross-border communities. They describe three of the theories and propose a new theory that fills in the gaps left by the other two. This article reviews the literature in a unique way. Future researchers should consider validating the model through an empirical study.

Ba (2001) asks what online social structures promote trust. Ba creates a social structure that should engender trust between on-line community members. They describe community as "the Holy Grail of the Internet." Ba describes how calculus-based trust becomes information-based trust. Information-based trust becomes transference-based trust. Ba lists barriers to trust and describes how reputation systems such as eBay's user ratings can help build calculus trust and make sellers more concerned about their reputation. However, in the online environment cheaters find it easy to create new on-line identities. Using third parties to manage reputation can help build trust. For further research, the authors suggest the following questions: What control structures best promote trust? How does the structure impact the agent's trust of the community? What is the life-cycle of a community? How does it begin, evolve and die? What attributes lead to a successful community? (Ba 2001) Future research should try to validate the game theory in some way with an empirical study.

Hahn, Moon and Zhang (2008) use Social Network Analysis to study the formation of OSSD (Open Source Software Development) teams. They analyzed data from real OSSD projects organized on SourceForge.net. They wanted to know what motivated developers to join specific teams. They discovered that developers tend to join projects initiated by people they already have ties with. Developers also tend to join projects that have teams with high-status developers. The authors suggest the following research questions: What role do the initiators and developers play in recruiting new developers? How does the joining process change over the life-cycle of the project? How does the process of developers joining a team change the structural characteristics of the network? Future researchers might use data from a different OSS development area. Additional research could examine how the process of team formation affects the overall success and sustainability of the project. (Hahn et al. 2008) Research might also examine the role corporate champions play in the formation and success of online communities of practice within an organization. This research might uncover a tension between the role of the corporate champions and the identity of the Community of Practice as a grassroots effort.

Gray (2004) performed an interpretive study of a community of practice set up for adult education program coordinators. The members of the community participated for following reasons: acquiring new skills and organizational policies, connecting with colleagues, reducing feelings of aloneness and isolation. The study also highlighted the importance of a group moderator to provide technical help, supporting group processes, facilitating the social aspect of the community and enhancing learning. Gray's research leads to the following questions. Gray (2004) discusses the role of the moderator in one particular group, but how does the role of the moderator change in different groups? How does the moderator's role change in different parts of the community life-cycle? How can communities avoid becoming victims of their own success, when the number of posts grow too high for people to read and respond to.

Trust

When group members feel they can predict the actions of the other group members and know they will not be taken advantage of, they are more likely to share knowledge in the community practice. Ibrahim and Ribbers (2009) examine the how trust impacts interorganizational systems. Ba (2001) creates an online social structure that should help community members trust each other. Chen and Hung (2010) suggest that trust influences knowledge contributing and knowledge collecting behaviors.

Ibrahim and Ribbers (2009) examine how competence and openness trust affect interorganizational systems, though they do not make the application to online communities of practice. They examine four types of Interorganizational Systems (IOS) resources: Human Knowledge, organizational domain-knowledge, business processes and IOS infrastructure. The authors suggest that future research might ask about additional types of trust, such as: credibility, benevolence and affect (Ibrahim et al. 2009). The authors performed three case studies. Additional research could use quantitative surveys to measure the user perception of trust. Their study deals with inter-organizational trust, but the same issues can exist within an organization as well. Their study does not specifically address online communities, but some of the concepts may be studied in that area.

In the context of e-commerce, Ba (2001) describes several levels of trust. Deterrent or Calculus-based trust means that someone acts in a trustworthy way because they fear the negative consequences of acting untrustworthily. Information-based trust allows members to predict the actions of the others because of their previous interactions with each other. Transference-based trust allows trust means that if one member trusts another member, the member can trust any third parties trusted by the intermediary (Ba 2001).

Ba (2001) asks what online social structures promote trust. Ba creates a social structure that should engender trust between on-line community members. They describe community as "the Holy Grail of the Internet." Ba describes how calculus-based trust becomes information-based trust. Information-based trust becomes transference-based trust. Ba lists barriers to trust and describes how reputation systems such as eBay's user ratings can help build calculus trust and make sellers more concerned about their reputation. However, in the online environment cheaters find it easy to create new on-line identities. Using third parties to manage reputation can help build trust (Ba 2001).

In face-to-face communities of practice, members learn to trust each other through a series of interactions. Trust in online communities is more challenging because the members often never see each other and even online interactions may be infrequent. Online community members are more likely to share knowledge when they believe they can rely on the other members of the community to provide honest, accurate information and not misuse information they are given. Chen and Hung suggest that trust significantly predicts knowledge contributing behaviors and knowledge collecting behaviors (Chen et al. 2010).

Perceived Enjoyment and a Sense of Belonging

Lu, Phang and Yu (2011) evaluated virtual communities to see why people continue to participate in them. They used usability and sociability theory to posit that perceived enjoyment and a sense of belonging determine a member's intention to continue to use a virtual community. The following things drive these factors: information service quality, interaction support, quality incentive policy, event organization, and leaders' involvement. The authors define perceived usefulness as an individual's opinion about whether or not using a particular technology will increase their job performance. Perceived usefulness was not supported by their research. They define perceived enjoyment as the extent to which the user enjoys using the system, regardless of the other benefits. They describe a sense of belonging as the social aspect of being a part of something. They break usability down into information service quality and interaction support quality. Information service quality describes the extent to which the members can easily find the information that they need. They describe interaction support quality as the ease with which members can communicate with each other. They break sociability down into the incentive policy, event organization and leaders' involvement. The incentive policy describes how the community recognizes and rewards contributions. Event organization describes activities the leadership organizes to get members to interact with each other. Leaders' involvement may include actions by members in addition to the group moderator such as active members and opinion leaders. Leaders can serve as knowledge resources, encouragers and shapers of content, enforcing group norms and building a healthy environment.

Individual Motivations can have a dramatic influence on the behavior in online communities of practice through the mechanism of Social Capital, including trust and the perception of reciprocity, and the perception of enjoyment and belongingness.

Chapter Three: Community Factors

Community factors include group moderation and turnover levels. Researchers have proposed factors which are critical for community success (Erat et al. 2006), proposed a life cycle for online communities (2009) and metrics which can be used to measure success (Preece 2001).

Other factors can include leadership effectiveness, interpersonal relationship and ideology of the community. Effective leadership can enhance knowledge sharing through enthusiasm, support and recognition of accomplishments. When the community environment facilitates the formation of interpersonal relationships, the members share knowledge with greater frequency. Members more frequently become involved with organizations that share their core sets of beliefs (Xu et al. 2009). Effective community policies, practices and enforced norms of behavior can encourage knowledge sharing (Cheliotis 2009; Silva et al. 2008). Having members post profile information and make relevant posts also increase the likelihood of knowledge sharing (Silva et al. 2008). Positive social influence from the community to share knowledge should also contribute to knowledge sharing (Posey et al. 2010). When communities and members share ideology, members share more knowledge (Cheliotis 2009).

The following factors can also encourage knowledge sharing in online communities of practice. Voluntary membership enhances knowledge sharing. Practical knowledge that validates the practices of the members can encourage knowledge sharing. Communities where the knowledge represents best practices within the industry encourage the members to share their knowledge. Communities where the members do not compete with each other encourage the sharing of knowledge. Asynchronous communication enables knowledge sharing because the ability to participate in the discussion does not require the members to log on to the system at the same time (Hara et al. 2007). Knowledge sharing increases when a moderator enforces the rules of the community (Gray 2004; Hara et al. 2007; Silva et al. 2008). Turnover can have a mixed affect on knowledge sharing within a community of practice. Communities need fresh members in order to keep from stagnating. However, the collected knowledge of the group declines when members spend less time in the community (Butler 2001; Ransbotham et al. 2011).

Erat, Desourza and Kurzawa (2006) examine Business Customer Communities. They perform initial research to describe the communities and the challenges they face in their formation. They briefly summarize the history of marketing in the Internet age. They quote Lave and Wenger's definition of a community of practice as a space where members share their activities and what it means for them and the community. They describe three types of external communities: Customer cross border communities, private customer communities and external business customer communities. A group of selected customers and employees who meet to share knowledge to create new products and services make up customer cross-border communities. Critical challenges for CBCs include internal acceptance, customer identification, incentives, trusting relationships, communication, and knowledge capture. When hosted by a firm, groups of customers who share information and opinions about the vendor form private customer communities. Challenges include sustainable membership levels, communication, belonging, trust, and knowledge transfer from customers. The vendor typically starts business customer communities and solicits information over the long term from other organizations which consume the product or function within the supply chain. The authors describe the differences between these types of communities.

The authors list four phases in the formation of a community: Preparing, planning, initiating, and sustaining. They also list a large number of Business Customer Community Critical Success factors and divide them into people, knowledge, and technology. People factors in online community success include the following. Find a leader. Find collaborative members. Look for solutions where everyone "wins". Avoid areas that may lead to conflict. Solicit help from stakeholders. Expect membership levels to change over time. Community roles should be revolving positions. Use new members to keep the discussion going.

Knowledge factors in online community success include the following. Select a topic for the community with importance for the members. Plan for the knowledge to be shared and implement the plan. Seek out multiple perspectives. Draft guidelines for member interaction and knowledge sharing. The environment should encourage informal interactions. Discuss openly difficulties about the topic environment. List gains in knowledge as they are achieved. Encourage members to record their experiences in the community. Reexamine the area of knowledge considered to be part of the topic. Cooperate and coordinate with communities on similar topics. Select a board of advisors for the community.

Hara and Hew (2007) used an in depth case study to see how nurses shared knowledge in an online community of practice. The nurses engaged in the following activities: Knowledge Sharing, and Solicitation. Nurses shared the following types of knowledge: institutional practice, and personal opinion. The following factors engender sustaining knowledge sharing: self-selection, validation, best practices, non-competition, asynchronous communication, and moderated discussion.

DeSanctis, Fayard, Roach and Lu (2003) examine how new technologies impact learning communities. They describe three case studies of various learning environments and describe three types of online learning communities: information kiosks, associations and communities of practice. They close with a handful of guidelines for online learning communities. This article approached the topic from a management perspective rather than an information systems perspective. The authors suggest that future researchers use the same process on other learning environments rather than the three described in this study (DeSanctis et al. 2003).

Wasko, Teigland and Faraj (2009) examine the social structures in communities of practice. They use the theory of collective action and the theory of public goods. They performed a social network analysis and conducted a survey. Their paper contains good descriptions of networks of practice as well as a good survey. General exchange and a "Critical Mass" of members sustains the NOP

(Network of practice).

Individuals more frequently form a relationship with the community as a whole than with a particular individual in the community. Expert members with more experience contribute more knowledge and more resources make the most contributions because they desire to increase their reputation. The core membership creates and maintains the knowledge store. Despite turnover, the pattern of exchange is consistent over time. They suggested that future research might include using a different network of practice or a different medium. They also suggested performing a longitudinal study over time. They also wondered how the "critical mass" of core users forms initially and how they create the "public good". They future research might uncover why some members "Freeload". They also wondered about the "shape" of the core community and which shapes operate most effectively (Wasko et al. 2009). Another interesting question might also include how the community leadership can change the "Shape" of the community.

Role of the Moderator

Campbell, Fletcher and Greenhill (2009) researched the role of conflict in the formation and reformation of a community's identity. They examined the concepts of power and identity from a critical, interpretive perspective with an ethnographic study. They used the theory of contemporary tribalism to describe how conflict defines and aligns the ideals and values held by online communities. They compare and contrast three roles of conflict within the community: Big Man, sorcerer, and trickster. The authors quickly explain that the term "big man" is meant to be gender-neutral and describes a community leader who has reached a preeminent position because of his or her status and wealth and must maintain the respect of the community to continue leadership. Often the "big man" maintains his or her position of power through the giving of gifts that the other members of the "tribe" are obligated to receive. According to literature on tribes, "sorcerers" are community members who set themselves apart from the rest of the community and gain power by generating conflict within the organization. Sorcerer's rarely support the leadership of the big man, unless there is a direct benefit to them. The authors describe the "trickster" as someone who attempts to manipulate people in the group for reasons known only to themselves. Often, they manipulate other members and cause conflict just to see if they can do so. The last group of members includes those members who do not typically engage in conflicts within a group. They accept the informational gifts provided by the Big Man and do not undermine his support among the other members.

Other approaches might include using a more quantitative approach. New research could use Tribal Theory to find the other roles in online communities. Research could validate their work using a different type of community of practice. Additional research might answer the following questions. What types of conflict occur within a community? How can communities avoid bad conflict and encourage good conflict? What roles do moderators play in mediating conflict between members?

Silva, Goel and Mousavidin (2008) researched the cohesiveness of community blogs. They used the theory base for communities of practice to find the following things that influence cohesion:

membership ground rules, moderators, profile information, good conduct, relevant posts, and group discipline. This article has a quick review of communities of practice literature as well as some information about blog research. Since Silva, et al performed an interpretive analysis of Metafilter posts, how might a different community or a different methodology change the results?

Wareham and Robey (2007) use the theory of social disorganization to describe how on-line auctions fight fraud within their communities. Crime occurs more often in weak, disorganized communities. Members with an attachment to the community most often fight crime in the community. They also describe how the stages of community development occur online and draw distinctions between formal and informal control structures. They did in-depth case studies of on-line communities. They also did a quantitative study of several internet forums and conducted personal interviews with members who fought fraud. They found that communities tend to enforce rules differently than outside authorities, and that communities more effectively prevent crime than traditional authorities. They encourage law enforcement organizations to work with communities to establish "Clan" control within the communities. They suggest that future research address how leaders and members create advanced, interdependent communities. They also suggest longitudinal studies to see how these factors change over time. They use the social disorganization theory and suggest the incorporation of other theories as well (Wareham et al. 2007).

Hara and Hew (2007) used an in depth case study to see how nurses shared knowledge in an online community of practice. Most of the members perceived that the moderator had an essential role to play. The moderator assisted new members who did not know the system. The moderator of the listserv screened requests for membership as well as requests to post messages to the Listserv. Screening the messages kept the messages on-topic and professional. This also allowed the moderator to enforce "netiquette". They suggest that future research might include confirmatory studies with other types of online communities of practice to ensure the generalizability of their findings. Interdisciplinary research might reveal how the six factors they describe apply in different fields? Research into the online community life cycle might show how the different stages affect how members share knowledge. They also suggest investigating the differences between sponsored communities and communities which emerge naturally. They also suggest an empirical validation of their model. (Hara et al. 2007)

Gray (2004) discusses the role of the moderator in a community of practice. The moderator made herself available. She helped members learn the technology. She managed the flow of the discussion by making posts when members did not, by posting questionnaires, surveys, resources and playing "devil's advocate". She refocused the threads to make sure they contained learning opportunities for the members. She encouraged members to post and thanked them when they did. She helped the members form a social community by providing emotional support and creating threads which unrelated to the work environment. She also scheduled "live" synchronous events.

Turnover

Butler (2001) created a Resource-based theory of sustainable social structures through an empirical study of LISTServe information. Benefits like information, influence and social support attract members to a community and encourage them to stay. Members of the community create a social structure by giving of their energy and time. Communities survive by creating benefits with greater value than the costs associated with the community. The community must transform the resources contributed into the community into tangible benefits for the members. Communities with large memberships can have a number of advantages by having increased resources. However disadvantages come from a less closely knit group, and a smaller percentage of users contributing to the group. The group must communicate at some level for the group to function, but an excess of communication activity makes a member consider leaving the group. The interaction of the membership size and communication activities create sustainable communities. Butler suggests that future research compare online communities to other types of communities. He also suggests that researchers add demographics, group composition, structure and communication processes. He also suggests that different types of community environments may have different results. For instance: push vs. pull technology, moderated groups, or groups that screen members. Also, do sponsored communities have different characteristics (Butler 2001)?

Ransbotham and Kane (2011) propose a two stage collaboration model in their quantitative study of featured articles on Wikipedia. First, the community must create knowledge. Second, the community must retain knowledge, which involves knowing which information to retain and which has become obsolete. The community has different needs in each stage. In general, moderate turnover in a community can have advantages. However, most communities get more turnover than they need. The authors suggests future research examine how critical factors may change when the group creates or retains knowledge (Ransbotham et al. 2011).

Mayer applies the field of economics to social networks. He argues that the stochastic models of economics describe social networking. People weigh the cost and benefit of their decisions. He suggests that social networks lead to improved flow of information. Social networks lead to increased market segmentation. Network size can affect pro-social behavior (Mayer 2009).

De Valck, van Bruggen and Wierenga (de Valck et al. 2009) use the field of Marketing to examine interactions in online communities. They used an online survey and a "netnography" of community observation and interviews. They describe six types of members: Core members, Conversationalists, Informationalists, Hobbyists, Functionalists, and Opportunists. The authors suggest the future research might use a more precise definition of activities conducted online. (de Valck et al. 2009) Future researchers might apply these types of users to communities of practice. Future research might also examine how groups encourage members to become core members.

Trier (2008) proposes dynamic analysis of social networks to support "static" social network analysis. Trier's article contains good information about Social Network Analysis. It also contains the names of a number of graphing software packages.

Critical Success Factors

Erat, Desouza, Schafer-Jugel, and Kurzawa (2006) suggest the following "Critical Success Factors" necessary to build, manage and sustain Business Customer Communities. The divide them into three dimensions: People, Knowledge and Technology. They did exploratory research using interviews and observation. They suggest the following additional research questions.

The people dimension includes the following factors: Leadership, collaborative membership, "win-win" thinking, willingness to work through conflict, stakeholder involvement, membership fluctuation contingency planning, rotation of community roles, new member recruitment.

The knowledge dimension includes the following factors: critical topic, vision for knowledge implementation, varying perspectives, codes for participation, informal interaction context, open discussion of challenges, record achievement of knowledge gains, experience capture, clarification of existing knowledge domain, cross community interaction, and formation of advisory board.

The technology dimension includes the following factors. Technology coverage, technology leadership, technology championing, training, transparency, ownership, privacy, channel use guidelines, event planning, document planting, and news updates. The authors suggest some of the following questions for future research. What role does leadership play in encouraging knowledge sharing? What role does the sponsoring organization play in the online community? They also suggest confirmatory empirical testing to establish a link between performance and the level of knowledge sharing and the link between knowledge sharing and the community culture, technology, and standards, (Erat et al. 2006) Researchers could perform this type of empirical testing to compare different kinds of communities of practice. For instance, how does a BCC (Business Customer Community) differ from a CBC (Customer cross-border community) or a PVC (professional virtual community)?

Community Life Cycle

Iriberri and Leroy (2009) propose critical success factors for each phase in the life cycle of online communities: Inception, Creation, Growth, Maturity and Death. They define various types of online communities and delineate various benefits provided by online communities. They suggest five stages of community life and different types of communities. They also review different metrics researchers use to define success. Lastly they divide the success factors between the stages of the life cycle and types of online communities.

They suggest the following metrics from their literature review: volume of member's contributions and quality of relationships between members, measures related to sociability (participants, message rate, satisfaction, perception of reciprocity and trust) and usability (interface errors, productivity, satisfaction), and quantitative and qualitative measures. Iriberri and Leroy suggest the following questions for future research. Researchers could test empirically to determine if the guidelines appropriately direct communities in particular stages. Do different types of users need different types of things? How can Communities of Practice implement these factors to ensure optimal development and success (Iriberri et al. 2009)? What metrics can researchers use to determine a community's current phase?

Online Community Success Metrics

Preece (2001) proposes several metrics to judge success in online communities. Preece divides these into Sociability and Usability. Sociability has to do with practices that encourage users to interact socially online. Purpose, people and policies build sociability. *Purpose* describes the reason the community exists. Purpose metrics measure the quantity and quality of messages and their relevance, and interaction and reciprocity between members. *People* describes the people in the group and the roles they adopt. *People* metrics include number and types of people who participate in the group and their various roles, user experience, age, gender, particular needs. *Policies* describe the formal and informal rules the group members follow. Metrics analyze the policies in place and their effectiveness, and the extent to which they encourage relationships. Usability describes the relative ease with which the users can begin to use the various facets of the system. Usability studies often examine user learning curve, user productivity, user satisfaction, user knowledge retention and errors made by user. Preece splits usability into the following: support for interaction, navigation, design of information, and access. *Support for interaction* describes how easily users can communicate. Metrics include the learning curve for interaction tools, the amount of time to send or receive a message, user satisfaction, retention and errors. *Design of information* describes the ease with which users can process the information about the community. Metrics include length of time to find information or perform information-related tasks, user satisfaction, user information retention,   and user information access errors. *Navigation* describes the ease with which members can move through the site to find the information they need. Preece suggests the following metrics: learning curve for navigation, time for user navigation, navigation information retention, user satisfaction and navigation errors. *Access* describes the ubiquity of the platform for users with various hardware and connection speeds. Metrics include software component access, download time, average response time, and software problems. Additional research would include comparing the proposed metrics to success measured with other methods such as ethnographies or questionnaires (Preece 2001). Future research could also tie these metrics with the community life cycle so that communities can determine their stage. Also, the metrics should be specifically worded for use in surveys. Several communities could be surveyed to give comparison numbers.

Toral, Martinez-Torres, Barrero and Cortez (2009) use Social Networking Analysis to determine what factors into success of online communities. They propose cohesion of the network, community core, and centrality of the network as antecedents of community success. They measure "success" by the number of active developers, the overall size of the community and the number of threads within the community.

A large number of community factors have been proposed as influencing the success of online communities of practice, including: the moderator's role, the rate of turnover, a number of critical success factors, the life cycle of the community and metrics which can be used to measure online community success.

Chapter Four: Technology Factors

The technological artifacts used to create the online community of practice can also play a part in the ability and willingness of group members to share knowledge. Important factors can include the ability for members to communicate asynchronously (Hara et al. 2007), and to present the desired "identity" to the group (Ma et al. 2007).

Erat, Desourza and Kurzawa (2006) examine Business Customer Communities and describe technology factors in online community success including the following. Technology should cover needs as they exist. The community leader should understand and guide the technology. The leader should "sell" the technology to the community. Technology should be demonstrated and members should be trained. Clarify the interests of the sponsoring organization. Make sure members know they will "own" the content they contribute. Do not capture member personal information. Create guidelines for when to use different communications media. Schedule times for the community to meet together online. Make documents about the network available to members. Update members with community news using newsletters.

Asynchronous Communication

Hara and Hew's (2007) case study into a nursing community of practice revealed, among other things, that the ability to communicate asynchronously is key to the success of knowledge sharing within a community of practice. Synchronous communication happens when users communicate directly in the same time frame. Asynchronous communication allows users to communicate outside of a specific time frame. An online chat system exemplifies a synchronous communication because it requires that both users engage in the same time frame. Email exemplifies asynchronous communication because messages do not require that members log in simultaneously.

Identity Verification

Ma and Agarwal (2007) examine knowledge contribution in online communities. They suggest that the ability to communicate identifying information and verify that information motivates knowledge contribution. Such communication leads to benefits such as recognition and increased self-worth. The ability to communicate identity in the desired way affects knowledge contribution directly and indirectly through satisfaction. They define identity as a member's self-assessment of various aspects of themselves such as intelligence, physical presence, personality, and motivating factors. They further define identity communication as how someone strives to portray their identity to other people. Goffman's self-presentation theory suggests that people put their need to present their identity ahead of goals that might bring people together. Identity communication is important in online communities for three reasons. First, members acquire information more efficiently when they can identify the experts. Second, people with similar identities form relationships with greater frequency. Third, communication of identifying information enables the knowledge contribution process. The theory of self-verification, which grew out of cognitive dissonance theory, suggests that people participate in interpersonal relationships when they feel the group recognizes and verifies their identities. The authors conceptualize perceived identity verification as how someone perceives the group sees their identity. Factors which may influence perceived identity verification include the amount of time the member has belonged to the community and the extent to which the members interact in real-world settings. The following things affect knowledge contribution: the member's identification with the group, the extent to which the group meets the informational needs of the member, length of time in the group and real-world interaction with other group members.

Virtual Copresence

Virtual copresence happens when group members get the sense that they share the same space with other group members. Communities build virtual copresence by using synchronous communication tools like chat or instant messenger as well as displaying the members online and their activities.

Persistent Labeling

Persistent Labeling builds identity verification by requiring that all of a member's interactions with the online community occur under the same user name. However, their data did not reveal a significant relationship between persistent labeling and knowledge contribution.

Self-Presentation

Self-presentation allows members to share their perception of their identities with other group members. Online communities achieve this through the selection of a user name, a signature on posts, a profile picture / avatar or nickname, member profile, link to personal web pages, or tools which build interactivity.

Deep Profiling

Deep profiling allows new users to select the most influential members in the group so they can know who to approach for information. Communities achieve this through membership directories, giving group members rankings or reputation scores, eliciting feedback, listings of actions by various members and the ability to search archived information in the online community.

Ma and Agarwal suggest a number of possible research questions. First, they only studied two online communities. Future research could include more online communities. Second, they used a cross-sectional study design which does not reveal causation between constructs only correlation. Future research might use a longitudinal study or an experimental design to find causal relationships in between the constructs. Third, they suggest a long-term study connecting perceived identity verification to activity and behavior of long-term members. Third, they suggest finding ways to more objectively measure deep profiling. Fourth, they suggest studying Identity Verification and Virtual Teams and computer mediated knowledge creation and dissemination. Fifth, they suggest studies consider what would make better virtual copresence tools. Sixth, they suggest a study of differences between online identity and real world identity and the differences between them (Ma et al. 2007).

Among other important technological factors, the ability to communicate asynchronously and present a palatable identity to the other group can influence the success of an online community of practice.

Chapter Five: Conclusion

Online communities of practice can greatly enhance the knowledge sharing ability of people from various organizations, and locations. However, community leaders should not assume that members will automatically share knowledge, but will need to create an environment conducive to the communication of ideas. In academic research about online communities of practice, important knowledge sharing factors can be broken down into individual motivational factors, community factors, and technology factors (Erat et al. 2006).

Individual motivational factors are those factors which mainly concern the member's point of view and include the following perceptions by the member:

- When one member shares knowledge, other members will respond in kind (Chang et al. 2010; Chen et al. 2010)

- Members have knowledge worth sharing (Chen et al. 2010)

- The benefit of the site is worth the costs of participating (Chen et al. 2010)

- Enjoyment when using the site (Lu et al. 2011)

- Feeling that one belongs to the community (Chen et al. 2010)

- Trust (Ba 2001)

- Value of individual rewards (Cheliotis 2009)

- Social capital (Robert et al. 2008)

Social capital describes the value of a member's social network and includes structural, relational and cognitive dimensions. The structural dimension of social capital describes the network of relationships between the group members. The relational dimension of social capital is how the member relates to the community as a whole. The cognitive dimension describes the language the members use to communicate (Chang et al. 2010).

Community factors describe the qualities of the online community and include the following factors:

- Community leadership from organizers and moderators (Hara et al. 2007; Xu et al. 2009)

- Rules and standards of behavior (Cheliotis 2009; Silva et al. 2008)

- Member profile information (Silva et al. 2008)

- Relevant knowledge sharing (Silva et al. 2008)

- Positive pressure from other members to share knowledge (Posey et al. 2010)

- Membership which is voluntary (Hara et al. 2007)

- Attracting new members at a rate which exceeds the loss of old members. (Butler 2001)

- The ease with which members can use the site and the ease with which they can create social ties with others. (Preece 2001)

Technology factors describe the technological capabilities of the platform used for the online community of practice and include the following factors. First, the community platform should have communication media which can take place over time and both users do not need to be logged on (Hara et al. 2007) Second, the platform should enable identity verification, which allows the member to present himself or herself in a way that is comfortable to them. Identity verification is made possible through technologies which enable members to feel they are in the same "space" as the other members, consistently make other members appear under the same user name, allow members to present themselves in a particular way through profile information, publishing profile information which allows members to see the expertise of the other members, (Ma et al. 2007)

Even though a great deal of research has been done about online communities and online communities of practice, much future research is still necessary. Since so many factors have been proposed as affecting the life of a community of practice, empirical, quantitative studies must be done to quantify these effects and determine which factors are most likely to play a part. Even with so many factors proposed, the experience in communities of practice is so varied that qualitative studies will still uncover additional factors which have not yet been proposed in the research. Since technological factors also play a part in the success of online communities of practice, additional information systems design research could create platforms which make it easier to collect, store and disseminate knowledge in these environments.

Part Two: Relevant Journal Articles

Below is a list of the journal articles reviewed. Many of these articles were used in the previous section. Since they were originally collected for the analysis of a topic they are summarized according to the Davis and Parker guidelines.

G.B. Davis and Clyde Parker (1997) suggested the following outline for a topic analysis: problem, importance of the research, theory base for research, significant prior research, possible research approach or methodology, potential outcomes of research and likelihood of each. These criteria were adapted and used to summarize the literature reviewed on online communities of practice. The articles were organized by theme, although often one article may contain several themes. The Title and the Reference are listed. The problem the research addresses and its relative importance are explained. The theoretical base and the research approach are shown. The results or outcomes of the study are listed along with suggested future research questions.

Auctions

Theme: Auctions

Reference: The Impact of Information Diffusion on Bidding Behavior in Secret Reserve Price Auctions (Hinz et al. 2008b)

Problem: How can sellers optimize their secret reserve price? How can buyers optimize their bidding price?

Importance of the Research: Allows buyers and sellers to more effectively manage online auctions

Theory Base: Information Diffusion

Research Approach: Authors created model and decision support system and performed a laboratory test of model and system.

Outcomes: Authors created \Online Auction Decision Support System. Authors propose that the buyer's social structure influences the estimate of the secret reserve price.

Future Research Questions: Their experiment assumes that agents always act the same way. How does false information impact the experiment? Test varying strategies by the Seller.

Theme: Auctions

Reference: Managing Information Diffusion in Name-Your-Own-Price Auctions. (Hinz et al. 2008a)

Problem: How does the "Secret" reserve price get communicated to bidders in an online auction?

Importance of the Research: Enables communication in online auctions.

Theory Base for Research: Information Diffusion and Social network Analysis

Research Approach: Laboratory Experiment

Outcomes: Bidders with many contacts access large amounts of information. "Bridge" Bidders that connect different parts of the network have dispersed information. Bidders in a strong "clique" have stale information.

Future Research Questions: Use a behavioral approach to this study rather than social network analysis. How does information overload affect the behavior of bidders? What incentives would encourage bidders to spread information?

Communities of Practice

Theme: Communities of Practice

Reference: Informal Learning in an Online Community of Practice (Gray 2004)

Problem: How can an online community of practice improve informal learning?

Importance of the Research: Informal learning leads to the sustainability of online communities

Theory Base: Communities of practice

Research Approach: Authors conduct an interpretive study of forty-three participants in an online community of practice. Data sources included forum postings, chat sessions, email, a participant survey, and interviews.

Outcomes: New Members learned the rules of the community of practice. Existing members learned their identity and the meaning of their work. The research tracked the formation of the identity of the members as well as the identity of the group. The community rewarded members in the following ways: Learning new skills and techniques, social connection, less isolation. The research highlighted the role of the moderator.

Theme: Communities of practice

Reference: Learning in Online Forums (DeSanctis et al. 2003)

Problem: What framework describes how electronic communication influences the learning process? How can participants form electronic networks?

Importance of the Research: Learning determines the success of learning communities

Research Approach: Authors examine tree case studies of different types.

Outcomes: Guidelines for collaborative learning.

Future Research Questions: Apply same process to other learning venues.

Theme: Communities of practice

Reference: The Provision of Online Public Goods: Examining Social Structure in an Electronic Network of Practice (Wasko et al. 2009)

Problem: What social structures make for good communities of practice?

Importance of the Research: Social structures help sustain communities of practice.

Theory Base: Collective Action and Public goods

Research Approach: The authors use Social Network Analysis and Survey.

Outcomes: General exchange and a "critical mass" of member support and sustain the network of practice. Members form a relationship with the community more often than a relationship with a particular individual. Expert members with more experience contribute more knowledge and more resources make the most contributions because they desire to increase their reputation. The core membership creates and maintains the knowledge store. Despite turnover, the pattern of exchange should remain consistent over time.

Outcome: Communities of practice create knowledge for the public good. More knowledge leads to continued participation.

Future Research Questions: Examine a different type of Network of practice or one using a different medium. Perform a longitudinal study over time. How did the critical mass form? How was the public good created? Why do free loaders use the resources without contributing? What is the shape of the core user group within the community? Which shapes lead to the best results?

Marketing

Theme: Viral Marketing, Social Network Analysis

Reference: The Effects of the Social Structure of Digital Networks on Viral Marketing Performance. (Bampo et al. 2008)

Problem: How do different social network structures affect the success of viral marketing campaigns? How can researchers model viral marketing campaigns? How can researchers simulate viral marketing campaigns in different types of social networks to see how a manager can make changes to the campaign in the early stages?

Importance of the Research: Impacts the effectiveness of viral marketing campaigns

Theory Base: Behavioral and Management science, "Viral" marketing campaign research.

Research Approach: The researchers created a simulation of a viral marketing campaign.

Outcomes: Model of viral marketing and guidelines for more effective viral marketing.

Theme: Marketing

Reference: Virtual Communities: A Marketing Perspective (de Valck et al. 2009)

Problem: How does the use of online communities affect their decision making processes? What patterns describe member participation within a virtual community? How do the most active members participate in discussions?

Importance of the Research: The authors describe "Word of mouse" as a growing in significance as a market influence.

Theory Base: Marketing

Research Approach: The authors use an online survey and "Netnography" (ethnography on the Internet) of interviews and observations of community members.

Outcomes: They describe six types of members: Core members, conversationalist, informationalists, Hobbyists, functionalists, and opportunists.

Future Research Questions: Better definition of activities conducted online

Gregg Greer

Economics

Theme: Economics

Reference: Online Social Networks in Economics (Mayer 2009)

Problem: How does economic theory describe social networks?

Importance of the Research: Enables organizations to match workers to jobs and attain educational goals.

Theory Base: Economics and Stochastic models (People weigh the cost and benefit of their decisions)

Research Approach: Authors conduct a literature review.

Outcomes: Social networks lead to improved flow of information. Social networks lead to increased market segmentation. Network size can affect pro-social behavior.

Future Research Questions: What influences the Individual's Motivations? How can communities build trust?

Self Disclosure

Theme: Self-disclosure

Reference: Proposing the Online Community Self-Disclosure Model: The Case of Working Professionals in France in the U.K. Who Use Online Communities. (Posey et al. 2010)

Problem: Why do people self-disclose in on-line communities? Study specifically examines a cross-cultural setting.

Importance of the Research: Businesses can market to people who self-disclose their details on social networking.

Theory Base: Social Exchange Theory, Social Penetration Theory, Individualism versus collectivism theory

Research Approach: Market research firm randomly selected Facebook users. Researchers went out of their way to avoid using college students. Researchers put math sections in an online website.

Outcomes: Positive social influence, reciprocity, trust increase Self-disclosure. Privacy risk perception decreases disclosure. Collectivism increases self-disclosure. The French are more individualistic than the British.

Future Research Questions: Include a wider conceptualization of anonymity. What other factors besides individualism and collectivism would influence how the cultures chose to disclose? If collectivism benefits online communities, how do communities reinforce it and reward it? The study contained self-reported responses and represents only one moment in time. So, a longitudinal or objective study may also shed some light on the phenomena. A longitudinal study could observe Social penetration. What are the other elements of Social Penetration Theory in addition to Satisfaction, stability and security in a relationship? Can organizations ethically get people to self-disclose so that they can market to them?

Interorganizational Communities

Theme: Interorganizational cross border collaboration

Reference: A Motivational model for technology-supported cross-organizational and cross-border collaboration (Romano et al. 2010)

Problem: How do organizations collaborate across-national borders?

Importance of the Research: Special issue editorial

Theory Base: Modified classification model of Chatterjee and Ravichandran, modified Lee Classification model, modified Kumar and Van Dissel classification, motivational model for technology-supported collaboration (proposed).

Research Approach: The authors perform a Literature Review

Outcomes: The motivational model for technology supported collaboration.

Future Research Questions: The authors suggest several gaps, but fill them with their Collaboration model. However, the research does not validate the new model with empirical research.

Knowledge Sharing

Theme: Knowledge Sharing, Individual motivations, Open Source Software development (OSS).

Reference: The Power of Gifts: Organizing Social Relationships in Open Source Communities (Bergquist et al. 2001)

Problem: Why do people contribute to Open Source Software Projects?

Importance of the Research: Management of open source software projects

Theory Base: "Classic" theories of gift-giving. New developments of old theories for the digital domain: socialization of new OSS developers, gift giving as a power structure, gift and giving as peer review.

Research Approach: Authors create an empirical test of theoretical foundations of gift-giving theory. Authors reviewed "official" OSS literature and compared against OSS newsgroups. Virtual Ethnography

Outcomes: The gift economy creates openness, and organizes relationships. OSS generates new ideas by giving gifts. The giver receives power by giving and uses it to guarantee code quality.

Theme: Knowledge Sharing, Social Capital, Individual motivations

Reference: Social Capital and Individual Motivations on Knowledge Sharing: Participant Involvement as a Moderator (Chang et al. 2010)

Problem: Why do people share knowledge in on-line communities?

Importance of the Research: Online communities exist to share knowledge.

Theory Base: Social Capital, Individual Motivation, and participant involvement

Research Approach: Quantitative: Results of a survey

Outcomes: Altruism, identification, reciprocity, and shared language positively influence knowledge sharing. Reputation, social interactions and trust had positive effects on quality, but not quantity of shared knowledge. Participant involvement moderates the relationship of altruism and the quantity of knowledge shared.

Outcome: Quantity and quality of shared knowledge

Future Research Questions: Conduct survey with a different demographic of members. Repeat study with different types of communities. Different types of communities may act in different ways. Since the Questionnaire was voluntary, "lurkers" may not have participated. People who do not participate may not understand their own motivations.

Theme: Knowledge Sharing, Individual Motivation, Community Factors, OSS Communities, Creative Commons Licensing, Rewards

Reference: From Open Source to Open Content: Organization, Licensing and Decision Processes in Open Cultural Production (Cheliotis 2009)

Problem: What similarities do OSS development communities share with communities that develop "cultural" content such as Wikipedia or Kompoz? What factors influence the type of Creative Commons licenses used under which circumstances?

Importance of the Research: Cooperative "Cultural" development projects are becoming more popular. What drives creators to use what types of licenses?

Theory Base: Framework based on Coase's Theory of the firm. Describes how OSS exist between individuals and companies.

Research Approach: Authors conducted a quantitative analysis of Creative Commons License usage.

Outcomes: Creation of decision tree and probabilities.

Future Research Questions: Examine of loosely coupled web services and application programming interface "mashups."

Theme: Knowledge Sharing, Individual motivations, Trust

Reference: To Give or to Receive? Factors Influencing Member's knowledge sharing and Community Promotion in Professional Virtual Communities (Chen et al. 2010)

Problem: Why do people share knowledge in PVCs (Professional Virtual Communities)? How do professional virtual communities differ from an online community of practice?

Importance of the Research: Knowledge sharing lies at the heart of why people form Professional Virtual Communities.

Theory Base: Factors which influence the increase of community knowledge

Research Approach: Structured Equation Modeling of data gathered from people in two virtual communities

Outcomes: Reciprocity, trust, knowledge sharing self-efficacy, and perceived relative advantage positively affect knowledge sharing. Knowledge contributing and collecting positively influence knowledge utilization. Knowledge collecting affects community promotion. Knowledge contributing effected community promotion in a limited way.

Future Research Questions: Data came from only two virtual professional communities. Repeat study with more communities. Perform a longitudinal study over the life cycle of a PVC. How does the level of knowledge activity influence the financial contribution of the PVC?

Theme: Knowledge Sharing, Community Factors, Business Customer Communities or External Communities

Reference: Business Customer Communities and Knowledge Sharing: Exploratory Study of Critical Issues. (Erat et al. 2006)

Problem: What challenges face Business Customer Communities (BCC's) and how can communities overcome them?

Importance of the Research: Enables businesses to communicate with customers

Theory Base: Customer community literature

Research Approach: The authors conduct a thorough case study of Lilly Critical Care Europe (Exploratory and descriptive research) Analysis of interviews and observations

Outcomes: Authors list a large number of BCC Critical Success factors and divide them into people, knowledge, and technology groups.

Future Research Questions: What role does leadership play in knowledge sharing? What role does the sponsoring organization play? Future researchers could conduct confirmatory testing including culture, technology, standards, etc. Does the performance of the group increase as the level of knowledge sharing increases?

Theme: Knowledge sharing, Individual motivation, Rewards

Reference: The Ties that Bind: Social Network Principles in Online Communities (Ganley et al. 2009)

Problem: How does a website get the members to generate high quality content? How do relationship and reputation relate to the social network?

Importance of the Research: How do communities encourage content generation with only virtual rewards? Research would allow social networking sites to optimize the relationship between reputation and the network

Theory Base: Social Capital, Structural Holes, and Reputation systems

Research Approach: Quantitative analysis of the network on Slashdot.

Outcomes: Proposed changes to mechanism that will increase ability to make money. Between-ness, constraint, participation and investment all influence Karma. "Karma" Score

Future Research Questions: More extensive data collection. Create Qualitative surveys for a topical examination of relationships. How does theory about basic organizational structure transfer into the online arena?

Theme: Knowledge Sharing, Community Factors, Community of practice

Reference: Knowledge-sharing in an Online Community of Health-Care professionals (Hara et al. 2007)

Problem: Knowledge sharing by nurses in an on-line community of practice. Sustaining knowledge sharing

Importance of the Research: Examines how communities of practice function across organizations. The coding method used for interviews and observations can gage current activities. The six proposed factors can improve new or existing communities of practice.

Theory Base: Communities of Practice

Research Approach: The authors conducted a qualitative, in depth, mixed method case study. Authors used online observation, interviews and analysis the contents of online messages.

Outcomes: Study highlights the role of the moderator. Study researches knowledge sharing, and solicitation. Communities share the following types of knowledge: Institutional practice and personal opinion. Communities sustain knowledge sharing through self-selection of members, validation of practices, sharing best practices, practicing non-competition, using asynchronous communication, and moderating discussions.

Future Research Questions: Use other communities of practice to confirm that six factors apply across other disciplines. Determine the relative importance of each factor during the community life cycle.

Theme: Knowledge Sharing, Created communities and emergent communities, Empirical examination of research model, knowledge sharing

Reference: The Interaction Between Knowledge Codification and Knowledge-Sharing Networks (Liu et al. 2010)

Problem: How can knowledge codification and knowledge sharing networks combine for effective Knowledge Transfer?

Importance of the Research: Combined method may work better than either method by itself

Theory Base: Knowledge management theory, Formal modeling of networks, Formal Game Theory

Research Approach: The authors construct a mathematical model based in game theory.

Outcomes: Knowledge codification stores knowledge in electronic databases for retrieval and use. Codification works best with explicit knowledge. Members receive tangible rewards. Knowledge sharing networks connect people and allow them to share knowledge through interpersonal relationships. Knowledge sharing works best with tacit knowledge. Members receive intangible, social rewards. When a community has codification and sharing networks, members may "hoard" codified knowledge to bolster their social network. When people will probably need to share again, use sharing networks (low codification rewards) and codification (high codification rewards).

Future Research Questions: How does knowledge sharing and knowledge contribution affect other knowledge management issues like knowledge creation?

Theme: Knowledge sharing, Individual Motivations, Community Factors

Reference: Volunteers' Involvement in Online Community Based Software Development (Xu et al. 2009)

Problem: Why do people contribute to Open Source Software Projects?

Importance of the Research: Management of Open Source Software Projects

Theory Base: Their research model incorporates individual motivations and community factors as drivers for involvement which drives performance.

Research Approach: Empirical analysis of data received from volunteer OSS developers.

Outcomes: Involvement determines performance. The following individual motivations drive involvement: personal software needs, expectation of increased skills and reputation, and enjoyment. Project community also plays a part with factors such as the effectiveness of the leadership, interpersonal relationship, and the ideological basis of the community.

Future Research Questions: Similar research in another OSS environment. Authors did not track which projects failed or successfully concluded.

Moderation

Theme: Moderation

Reference: Conflict and identity shape shifting in an online financial community. (Campbell et al. 2009)

Problem: What role does conflict play in the formation and reformation of a community's identity

Importance of the Research: Community design and governance

Theory Base: Contemporary Tribalism

Research Approach: Researchers adopt a "Broadly Ethnographic", Critical Interpretive perspective (Power and identity).

Outcomes: Conflict can define and align the ideals and values held by a community

Future Research Questions: Research can validate theory using other approaches. Research may be able to find other roles besides, big man, sorcerer and trickster.

Theme: Moderation, Community Factors, Communities of practice

Reference: Exploring the Dynamics of Blog Communities: The Case of MetaFilter (Silva et al. 2008)

Problem: What makes a community blog cohesive?

Importance of the Research: Cohesive communities function better.

Theory Base: Communities of Practice

Research Approach: Authors conduct an interpretive analysis of Metafilter posts.

Outcomes: Cohesion arises from membership ground rules, moderators, profile information, good conduct, relevant posts, and group discipline.

Future Research Questions: Future research can study of same issues in a different environment or study the same issues with a different method.

Theme: Moderation

Reference: The Role of online Trading Communities in Managing Internet Auction Fraud (Wareham et al. 2007)

Problem: Managing Fraud in online auction houses

Importance of the Research: Giving communities more effective ways of dealing with fraud

Theory Base: Social Disorganization theory: Crime occurs in "weak and disorganized" communities. Also members more attached to the community fight more crime. The theory delineates stages of community development and distinctions between formal and informal control.

Research Approach: The authors conduct a qualitative study of three case of on-line communities. The authors studied internet forums and conducted some personal interviews of individuals fighting fraud.

Outcomes: Communities enforce rules differently from the authorities. Interdependent, anticrime communities fight crime most effectively. Authorities should encourage cooperation and clan control.

Future Research Questions: What conditions lead to more advanced, interdependent communities? Future research should include longitudinal Studies to confirm. Future research could apply more community theories to on-line communities.

Networks of Practice

Theme: Network of Practice

Reference: Trans-situated Learning: Supporting a Network of Practice with an Information Infrastructure. (Vaast et al. 2009)

Problem: What learning dynamics emerge when people have similar jobs communicate in a community despite their separation by distance?

Importance of the Research: Important for the success of networks of practice

Theory Base: Situated Learning, Networks of practice, Information Infrastructures, Practice-based perspective of learning, Computer-mediated contexts

Research Approach: Authors prepared a case study of a web-based system in environmental health.

Outcomes: Model of trans-situated learning

Future Research Questions: How does model work when group members do not have close relationships or when practices of the community are more diverse? How does trans-situated learning affect other kinds of communities? What constructs could future researchers add to their model?

Theme: Networks of practice: Wikipedia

Reference: The Interplay between Digital and Social Networks (Arazy et al. 2011)

Problem: What determines the quality of team-produced articles on Wikipedia?

Importance of the Research: Quality is crucial to the survival of that resource and similar resources.

Theory Base: Research on Wikipedia, which, since it is in the beginning stages, is largely without established theories.

Research Approach: Authors performed a quantitative study of Wikipedia articles.

Outcomes: Membership diversity, healthy intra-team conflict and membership administrative and content generating roles drives the quality of Wikipedia team-produced articles.

Future Research Questions: What are additional methods for measuring quality of the articles? The research used information available on Wikipedia, but cannot account for information not stored on Wikipedia. How do these findings compare with the quality of knowledge in a community of practice?

Theme: Networks of practice: Wikipedia

Reference: Decentralization in Wikipedia Governance. (Forte et al. 2009)

Problem: How does an organization encourage and manage "Self" government?

Importance of the Research: This research may be illustrative of governance in other networks of practice.

Theory Base: Commons-based government.

Research Approach: The authors conducted qualitative research using interviews with Wikipedia workers.

Outcomes: Wikipedia uses highly organized norms, policies and rules. As it continues to grow, the governance becomes more decentralized.

Future Research Questions: What factors drive the choice of governance style of a community of practice?

Online Communities

Theme: Special Issue, Online Communities

Reference: The Interplay between digital and social networks. (Agarwal et al. 2008)

Problem: Editorial for special issue on digital and social networks.

Importance of the Research: Introduces topic and describes papers selected and the selection process.

Outcomes: Agarwal suggests three ways that digital social networks differ from real-world social networks: scale, communication dynamics, increase of user-generated content.

Theme: Online communities

Reference: The Impact of Community Commitment on Participation in Online Communities. (Bateman et al. 2011)

Problem: Why do people participate in online communities?

Importance of the Research: Helps people understand why people do or do not participate in their community.

Theory Base: Organizational commitment research which describes continuance, affective and normative commitments.

Research Approach: The authors developed model and then created a survey to test it.

Outcomes: New model

Future Research Questions: Future research can examine synergy effects from different kinds of commitment, the progression of commitment over time. How does the commitment by the people fit in to the overall functioning of the community? How does commitment fit with Kim's core-periphery structure? Their research use age, gender and tenure as moderating variables. Are there other variables which could moderate these relationships? How does the community socialize members? What are the antecedents for the various types of commitment? The authors suggest shared values, trust, and supportiveness from the previous research on community commitments, but do not attempt to support it.

Theme: Sustaining online communities

Reference: Understanding the Sustainability of a Virtual Community: Model Development and Empirical Test (Cheung et al. 2009)

Problem: Why do people continue to use online communities?

Importance of the Research: Important for sustainability

Theory Base: Information Systems continuance model, relationship marketing, the uses and gratifications paradigm and social influence theory.

Research Approach: The authors conducted a survey.

Outcomes: The intention to continue using and the intention to recommend are driven by satisfaction, commitment and group norms. Purposive value, self-discovery, entertainment value, social enhancement, and maintaining interpersonal interconnectivity drive the antecedents to these intentions.

Outcomes: Intention to continue using and intention to recommend in virtual communities

Future Research Questions: A longitudinal study might provide more information about how these concepts interact over time.

Theme: Online Communities

Reference: Through a Glass Darkly: Information Technology Design, Identity Verification and Knowledge Contribution in Online Communities. (Ma et al. 2007)

Problem: What makes members contribute knowledge in an online community?

Importance of the Research: Knowledge contribution is crucial to the success of online communities

Theory Base: Theory of perceived identity verification (which is taken from social psychology concepts of identity), Goffman's Self-presentation theory, the theory of self-verification, the theory of attribution.

Research Approach: The authors conduct an empirical study by surveying community members in two communities. The authors created and excellent literature review summary and a good explanation of how they did surveys to account for validity. They used the Twenty Statements Test (TST) created by Kuhn and McPartland, and Knowledge Contribution measures from Wasko and Faraj. They include many of their measures in the appendix.

Outcomes: Virtual Presence, Persistent Labeling self-presentation and deep profiling all affect the perceived identity verification which impacts satisfaction and knowledge contribution

Future Research Questions: They only studied two online communities. Future research might include a wider scope. The cross-sectional study design does not reveal causation only correlation. A longitudinal study or a experimental design might bring out causal relationships. They suggest a long-term study connecting perceived identity verification to activity and behavior of long-term members. They suggest finding ways to more objectively measure deep profiling. They suggest future research might create better virtual copresence tools. They also suggest that future researchers study the differences between online identity and real world identity and the differences between them.

Theme: Online communities

Reference: Usability and Sociability in Online Communities: A Comparitive Study of Knowledge Seeking and Contribution (Phang et al. 2009)

Problem: How do usability and sociability affect knowledge contributing and knowledge sharing in online communities?

Importance of the Research: Community success depends on knowledge sharing.

Theory Base: Work on online communities by Preece.

Research Approach: The authors conducted a quantitative Survey

Outcomes: The authors create a good model and a good literature review.

Theme: Open Source Software Communities

Reference: An Empirical Study of the Driving Forces behind Online Communities. (Toral et al. 2009)

Problem: What drives the success of communities?

Importance of the Research: What factors must be present for the success of online communities? How can researchers define success?

Theory Base: Social Network Analysis

Research Approach: The authors use social network analysis

Outcomes: Network cohesion, core of the community, network structure and network centrality drive success in online communities. The authors measured "success" by the number of active developers, community size and the number of "threads".

Future Research Questions: What is an appropriate definition of success for an online community of practice and how can it be measured?

Theme: Online communities Literature review

Reference: Virtual Worlds – Past, Present, and Future: New Directions in Social Computing. (Messinger et al. 2009)

Problem: How can researchers classify "virtual worlds"? What is the existing literature on virtual worlds? How does Second Life exemplify a virtual world?

Importance of the Research: The authors argue for the pervasiveness and potential of virtual worlds. They project that in five years, virtual communities will become as important to organizations as the World Wide Web is now.

Theory Base: They are reviewing literature to find the existing theory base for research into virtual worlds.

Research Approach: The authors do a mixed method study using literature review, case study and survey.

Outcomes: Taxonomy of types of virtual worlds by Purpose, Place, Platform, Population and Profit model. The researchers include a list of important "virtual worlds" used in games.

Future Research Questions: How does the appearance of the Avatar affect the interactions within the virtual world? How do people behave differently on-line than they do in the real world? How does an organization market to people in a virtual world? How should organization differentiate between marketing to the avatar and marketing to the real person behind it? How can organizations employ the best business models for virtual worlds? How can organizations conduct market research within and about virtual worlds? How can organizations market virtual services? How will retailing and ecommerce strategies differ between virtual worlds and the Internet? How can organizations manage their customer relationships within a virtual world? How can organizations use virtual worlds to enhance communication between employees? Can a community of practice exist in a virtual world? If so, how would it differ from a more traditional format?

Theme: Online Community success, Online community Life cycle

Reference: A Life-cycle Perspective on Online Community Success (Iriberri et al. 2009)

Problem: What critical success factors drive community success in each stage of online community development?

Importance of the Research: What are the critical factors for creating self-sustaining communities?

Theory Base: Thorough literature review of articles and the theories used in online community research.

Research Approach: The authors conduct a very thorough literature review.

Outcomes: Literature review for online communities.

Future Research Questions: Future research could create an empirical test to determine if their guidelines fit the life-cycle stages. Do different types of users have different needs? How can communities implement these factors to ensure optimal development and success?

Theme: Online community success

Reference: Sociability and Usability in Online Communities: Determining and Measuring Success. (Preece 2001)

Problem: How can people measure success in online communities?

Importance of the Research: Success must be clearly defined in order to set goals for achieving success in online communities.

Theory Base: Human Computer Interaction

Research Approach: The authors conduct a thorough literature review.

Outcomes: The authors create sociability and usability metrics for online communities.

Future Research Questions: Future research might compare success measures to perception of success. Future researchers might compare success and the perception of success across several communities.

Theme: Open source software projects

Reference: Understanding Sustained Participation in Open Source Software Projects. (Fang et al. 2009)

Problem: Why do people participate in Open Source Software (OSS) projects?

Importance of the Research: Participation is crucial for successful OSS projects.

Theory Base: Legitimate Peripheral Participation (LPP), Situated learning, and Identity formation

Research Approach: The researchers did qualitative research by conducting a longitudinal case study using multiple documents.

Outcomes: The factors that encourage members to join a group are different from the factors that make them stay. Situated learning and identity construction lead to sustained participation making conceptual and practical contributions.

Future Research Questions: Future research could empirically test the model or collect additional primary data by interviewing programmers. Future research could use quantitative surveys to make the results more generalizable. Future research might add community level factors to the model or examine how power and roles factor into participation. Future research might also use Bourdier's theory of practice.

Reviews

Theme: Reviews

Reference: Informational Cascades and Software Adoption on the Internet: an Empirical Investigation. (Duan et al. 2009)

Problem: How do Informational cascades affect software adoption? Users must often make adoption decisions without full information. When they do so by adopting someone else's decision, researchers call this an informational cascade.

Importance of the Research: Informational cascades can explain why on-line user reviews do not always work as well as why the user may make sub-optimal decisions.

Theme: Reviews

Reference: Examining the Relationship between Reviews and Sales: The Role of Reviewer Identity Discloser in Electronic Markets. (Forman et al. 2008)

Problem: How does the disclosure of a reviewer's identity influence the perception of the review?

Importance of the Research: Electronic commerce is greatly influenced by online reviews.

Theory Base: Research on Information Processing

Research Approach: The authors conduct a quantitative evaluation of Amazon data.

Outcomes: Customers viewed reviews with identity information more positively. Customers more positively viewed Reviews from a closer geographical location were more positively viewed.

Future Research Questions: Researchers found it difficult to measure member level identification. Future research might evaluate identity perceptions and use alternative analysis techniques or analyze the text of reviews. Future research might also use different data, a different vendor, or a different product.

Social Network Analysis

Theme: Social Bookmarking

Reference: Innovation Impacts of using Social Bookmarking Systems. (Gray et al. 2011)

Problem: How can social bookmarking systems increase employee innovativeness?

Importance of the Research: Essential to know if social bookmarking systems have value.

Theory Base: Social Networking Analysis

Research Approach: The authors conducted a Social Network Analysis of a social bookmarking system used by a company.

Outcomes: When someone is exposed to more information from different sources, they will see more novel information. The shape of a member's network determines the amount of novel information they see. "Bridges" over structural "holes" have an advantage.

Future Research Questions: The authors assumed that more bookmarks accessed led to more novel information, but future research might enable them to more directly measure novelty. Future research may link use of social bookmarking to other outcomes besides innovation or review the impact of information "silos" on the efficacy of social bookmarking. Future researchers could study additional factors in social bookmarking behavior such as: culture, roles, motivation, reputation, and benefits or find other ways to measure innovation. How can communities of practice draw in new members with information to share? How can communities draw information out of current members?

Theme: Social Network Analysis, Open Source Software

Reference: Emergence of New Project Teams from Open Source Software Developer Networks: Impact of Prior Collaboration Ties. (Hahn et al. 2008)

Problem: What motivates developers to join Open Software Development teams? How do they choose which ones to join?

Importance of the Research: Uncovers the factor that drive the formation of new OSSD teams.

Theory Base: Social Network Analysis

Research Approach: Authors analyzed real OSSD projects.

Outcomes: Developers join projects when they have ties with the initiator of the project. Developers join projects that have teams of developers of high status.

Future Research Questions: What role do the initiators and developers play in recruiting new developers? How does the joining process change over the life-cycle of the project? How does the process of developers joining a team change the structural characteristics of the network? How does the process of team formation affect the overall success and sustainability of the project? Future research might use data from a different OSS development area.

Theme: Social Network Analysis

Reference: Casting the Net: A Multimodal Network Perspective on User-System Interactions. (Kane et al. 2008)

Problem: How can researchers best describe the user-system relationship?

Importance of the Research: Research should explain the user interaction with the system. All prior research focused on "didactic" system usage instead of multi-modal networks.

Theory Base: Social Network Analysis

Research Approach: Authors conducted a survey of healthcare systems users

Outcomes: The centrality of the information system within the social network positively influences the efficiency and quality of information system. Information System centrality has to do with the indirect effect of the system on people who do not use the information system. The aggregated strength of the users' interactions with the Information System does not have an effect on efficiency or quality.

Future Research Questions: Future research could test the same theories in other environments. Longitudinal studies could study these relationships over time. This study assumes identical nodes on the network. How might the type of task or system affect the structure?

Theme: Social Network Analysis, Email

Reference: Towards Dynamic Visualization for Understanding Evolution of Digital Communication Networks. (Trier 2008)

Problem: Social Network Analysis has shortcomings and does not tell the whole story.

Importance of the Research: Allows for dynamic analysis of social networks.

Theory Base: Social Network analysis, Dynamic network Analysis

Research Approach: Authors Conducted a Longitudinal Study of Enron E-mail

Outcomes: Authors created an event-based dynamic network visualization protocol using Social Network Intelligence software ("Commetrix") and Graphvis (an open source graphics software package).

Future Research Questions: Future research might identify people of importance on the network by their activities and impact or study "catastrophes" and how they affect networking to form predictive models. Future research might create a new methodology for dynamic networking to generate new insights or algorithms to automatically detect community formation. Future researchers might combine network analysis with content analysis to study innovation diffusion in online communities. The software developed could be used to analyze communities of practice. Additional methods to show network change over time could be proposed.

Trust

Theme: Individual motivation: Trust

Reference: Establishing Online Trust Through a Community Responsibility System (Ba 2001)

Problem: What online social structures promote trust?

Importance of the Research: Trust enables transactions between members

Theory Base: Game Theory

Research Approach: Authors use Game Theory to prescribe social structures which promote trust between members.

Outcomes: New community responsibility system allows impersonal anonymous transactions. The buyer trusts the community, not the seller. The community takes action against the people who break the rules

Future Research Questions: What control structures work best? How does the structure impact the agent's trust of the community? What is the life-cycle of a community? How does it begin, evolve and die? What attributes lead to a successful community?

Theme: Trust

Reference: What Does the Brain Tell Us about Trust and Distrust? Evidence from a Functional Neuroimaging study. (Dimoka 2010)

Problem: How can researchers describe the nature of trust and distrust in impersonal E-commerce?

Importance of the Research: Knowing what makes people trust each other enables them to do business online.

Theory Base: Theories on trust. The authors found little research on distrust because researchers define distrust as the opposite end of the trust continuum

Research Approach: Authors performed an experiment measuring brain activity with functional neuroimaging tools.

Outcomes: Trust and distrust generate activity in different areas of the brain

Future Research Questions: The Seller profiles used do not represent real-world profiles. Further research might use real-world examples. What elements make up trust and distrust? Future researchers might use better technology to sense brain activity.

Theme: Trust, Interorganizational Systems

Reference: The Impacts of Competence-trust and openness-trust on interorganizational systems. (Ibrahim et al. 2009)

Problem: How do competence trust and openness trust affect the use of interorganizational systems?

Importance of the Research: Trust is crucial to the success of interorganizational systems. When investments outweigh resources, interorganizational relationships fail.

Theory Base: Resource-based view, Transaction-cost economics

Research Approach: Authors conducted three case studies of interorganizational relationships.

Outcomes: Openness trust and competence trust positively influence the use of human knowledge and organizational domain knowledge resources. Competence trust positively influences the usage of resources related to interlinking business processes.

Future Research Questions: Future researchers might use a quantitative approach with a survey, rather than a qualitative approach. Trust research delineates many different kinds of trust besides those studied. Additional research might cover credibility, benevolence and affect. Future research might also cover intraorganizational relationships or on-line communities.

Turnover

Theme: Turnover, Sustainable communities

Reference: Membership Size, Communication Activity and Sustainability: A Resource-Based Model of Online Social Structures. (Butler 2001)

Problem: How do communities create sustainable on-line social structures? How do size and communication activity influence each other?

Importance of the Research: Turnover is an important factor in the long-term success of online communities.

Theory Base: Resource-based theory of sustainable social structures. Membership size and communication activity interact to create sustainable communities

Research Approach: Author performed a quantitative analysis of Listserv information.

Outcomes: Size and communication activity can have positive or negative effects on the success of the online community. Communities must balance the two of these.

Future Research Questions: Future researchers might study the new theory outside of an online community or compare online community results to other types of communities. Researchers might develop the theory as an organizational theory using demographics, group composition and structure and communication processes. Researchers might conduct similar studies in differing environments. Would "pull" or "push" technology make a difference? Would using moderators or screening members have an impact? Researchers might review communities which operate within a larger organization – such as a community of practice at an organization.

Theme: Turnover

Reference: Membership Turnover and Collaboration Success in Online Communities: Explaining Rises and Falls from Grace in Wikipedia. (Ransbotham et al. 2011)

Problem: How can Wikipedia authorship teams generate collaborative efforts by reducing turnover?

Importance of the Research: Managing turnover is crucial to the success of any group activity. At first, turnover in a group improves knowledge creation and retention, but turnover inhibits the group after it reaches a certain threshold.

Theory Base: Kane's two stage collaboration model: creation stage and retention stage.

Research Approach: The authors performed a quantitative analysis of featured articles on Wikipedia

Outcomes: The authors found support for hypothesis and two stage model. The community's needs in each of the two stages can vary widely. Moderate levels of turnover helps the community – but communities typically get more turnover in the retention phase than they need.

Future Research Questions: Whether the group operates in creation or retention stage may change the characteristics which foster collaboration.

Virtual Communities and Virtual Teams

Theme: Virtual communities

Reference: Encouraging Participation in Virtual Communities through Usability and Sociability Development (Lu et al. 2011)

Problem: Why do people continue to use online communities?

Importance of the Research: Unless a community knows what factors drive its sustainability, it cannot hope to manage those factors.

Theory Base: Usability and sociability research, Technology Acceptance.

Research Approach: The authors created a quantitative survey.

Outcomes: Enjoyment and sense of belonging drive the intent to continue to participate. The research did not support usefulness. Information service quality, interaction support quality incentive policy, event organization and leaders' involvement influence enjoyment and a sense of belonging.

Theme: Virtual Teams ,Technology supported teams

Reference: Team Size, Dispersion, and Social Loafing in Technology-Supported Teams.
(Alnuaimi et al.)

Problem: What factors drive "social loafing" in virtual teams?

Importance of the Research: Virtual Teams must manage "social loafing" to be effective.

Theory Base: Moral Disengagement

Research Approach: The authors conducted a laboratory study. They assigned students to different groups and had them use group support software.

Outcomes: Team size and dispersion influence social loafing. Mediating factors include responsibility, blame, and dehumanization.

Future Research Questions: Future researchers could examine other tasks than brainstorming or not use students as subjects. Additional experiments might disperse teams geographically or use more than just a chat-based system. Social Loafing and Lurking behaviors impact online communities of practice. Future research might add other constructs such as self-efficacy to their model. How does social loafing behavior change over time?

Theme: Virtual Teams

Reference: Cognitive Conflict and Consensus Generation in Virtual Teams during Knowledge Capture: Comparative Effectiveness of Techniques. (Chiravuri et al. 2011)

Problem: How can virtual teams best capture knowledge and resolve conflicts between subject matter experts?

Importance of the Research: Effective knowledge management begins with knowledge capture. Virtual teams cannot use inconsistent knowledge.

Theory Base: Repertory Grid, Delphi

Research Approach: The authors conducted a field experiment with real subject matter experts.

Outcomes: In the short run, Delphi performed better at reducing conflict and increasing consensus. However in the long run the Repertory Grid system outperformed Delphi.

Future Research Questions: How do online communities of practice resolve conflicts?

Theme: Virtual Teams, Knowledge Integration

Reference: Social Capital and Knowledge Integration in Digitally Enabled Teams (Robert et al. 2008)

Problem: How does social capital behave differently in face to face and online settings?

Importance of the Research: Social capital affects the success of virtual teams.

Theory Base: Social Capital, Knowledge Integration

Research Approach: The authors conducted an experiment. They took forty-six teams which had worked together before and tracked how they performed face-to-face and over the Internet. The article lists the questions they asked.

Outcomes: Virtual teams found structural and cognitive social capital more important. Relational capital did not change between the environments. Knowledge integration affected the quality of the team's decisions.

Future Research Questions: Why do team members not integrate knowledge from other team members? The authors suggest that social capital plays a part. Future research might use non-student subjects. Future researcher might find another way to operationalize cognitive capital. Future researchers might use a similar experimental research method with a different theory. Future research might compare how teams with and without a history together perform. This experiment could have subjects interact online first and then face to face and vice versa.

Theme: Virtual Teams, Trust

Reference: The Role of Communication and Trust in Global Virtual Teams: A social Netowrk Perspective (Sarker et al. 2011)

Problem: What theories links performance, communication and trust in virtual teams?

Importance of the Research: Virtual teams need trust to function efficiently.

Theory Base: Trust theory: Additive, interaction and mediation trust.

Research Approach: The researchers did a social network analysis in an experimental environment. They created groups that worked together over time.

Outcomes: Trust concerns relationships more than individuals. Social network approaches to trust work better than individual attribute approaches.

Future Research Questions: Future research might use non-student subjects. The social network analysis only looked at degree centrality. Additional research could review other SNA roles. How would results differ if project team managers assigned reviews?

Theme: Virtual Teams

Reference: Vital Signs for Virtual Teams: An Empirically Developed Trigger Model for Technology Adaptation interventions. (Thomas et al. 2010)

Problem: How can leaders of virtual teams know when they need to change the way they use technology?

Importance of the Research: Keeping up with technology is important for the success of virtual teams.

Theory Base: Adaptive Structuration Theory, Team Information Communication Technology (ICT) adaptation. The authors create a five trigger model and the VT Leader ICT-Intervention conceptual framework.

Research Approach: The authors conducted interviews with practicing virtual team leaders using the critical incident technique.

Outcomes: The authors create a model with the following triggers: external and internal constraints, inadequate Information Communication Technology, inadequate Information Communication Technology Knowledge skills and abilities, inadequate trust and inadequate relationships.

Future Research Questions: Future research could extend existing work on conflict resolution and participation in information systems projects. How can team leaders assess the knowledge, skills and abilities of their team members when they never see them? Future researchers could create a list of the different types of contexts where combinations of triggers combine to initiate intervention. How do managers respond when multiple triggers present themselves? How does the critical incident interview technique apply to communities of practice? What critical triggers cause leaders in online communities of practice to change the way they use technology? Future research could survey members of communities of practice to see if they can confirm similar triggers.

Theme: Virtual teams and Social Networks

Reference: The Influence of Virtuality on Social Networks withing and Across Work Groups. (Suh et al.)

Problem: How does virtuality affect one's social network in a virtual workgroup? The authors define virtuality as using individual and group communication technologies. How does virtuality affect group connectedness and the communication of tacit knowledge.

Importance of the Research: Knowledge sharing is crucial to the success of virtual teams.

Theory Base: Computer-mediated communication theory, Proximity Theory, Social network theory

Research Approach: The authors surveyed global business consulting firms and did hierarchal linear modeling

Outcomes: Virtuality at the individual level increases the strength of intra-group ties and the network range of the extra-group. The level of group virtuality, dispersion and support affect virtuality on the individual level.

Future Research Questions: Future researchers could create a more detailed understanding of what virtuality means. The research used knowledge-intensive firms. Less knowledge-based firms might give different results. Future researchers might find a better way to measure social network bridges to other groups or examine how social networks relate to team performance. Future research might add more constructs to their model.

Theme: Virtual teams, trust

Reference: Individual Swift Trust and Knowledge-based Trust in Face-to-face and Virtual Team Members. (Robert et al. 2009)

Problem: What causes people to trust each other in virtual teams?

Importance of the Research: Trust is essential to functioning in virtual teams.

Theory Base: Theories about different types of trust: cognitive, initial, knowledge-based, presumptive, and swift

Research Approach: The authors conducted an experiment to see how trust formed.

Outcomes: The authors created a two-stage model of how trust forms: Member characteristics and team member individual factors drive swift trust. Knowledge trust builds and swift trust fades as a members behaviors drive trust. Virtual teams failed more often, which meant that people were less likely to extend trust to future activities.

Future Research Questions: How does team diversity affect trust? What is the tipping point between swift trust and knowledge –based trust? How can one reduce the perceived risk of a virtual team? How do different media types affect knowledge-based trust?

Virtual Worlds

Theme: Virtual Worlds, Intention to purchase virtual products

Reference: An Odyssey into Virtual Worlds: Exploring the Impacts of Technological and Spatial Environments on Intention to Purchase Virtual Products. (Animesh et al.)

Problem: What makes consumers want spend real money to buy "virtual" products in a virtual world?

Importance of the Research: Virtual worlds must have some way of making money.

Theory Base: Stimulus Organism Response (S-O-R). Virtual Experience (tele-presence, social presence, and flow) drive intent to purchase. Technological and spatial environments drive experience.

Research Approach: The authors conducted a quantitative survey.

Outcomes: Interactivity drives telepresence and flow. Sociability drives social presence. Density and stability drive virtual experiences.

Future Research Questions: Future research might include more types of virtual worlds than Second Life. Researchers could use an experiment to determine if volunteer users differ from mandatory users. Intention to buy virtual goods may not represent the actual purchasing behavior, so future research could measure the difference between intention and action. Future research could examine trust, exploration, creativity, and learning and how the purchase of real goods differs from the purchase of virtual goods.

Theme: Virtual Worlds

Reference: Arguing the Value of Virtual Worlds: Patterns of Discursive Sensemaking of an Innovative Technology. (Berente et al.)

Problem: How do business professionals "make sense" of the usefulness of virtual worlds?

Importance of the Research: Good initial research to predict how organizations will use virtual world technology. The researchers apply grounded theory methodology and go into detail about the coding process.

Theory Base: Sensemaking and Touliminian analysis

Research Approach: Business professionals spent a dozen hours on Second Life and then wrote essays which the authors analyzed qualitatively

Outcomes: Authors found the following themes: "Confirmation, open-ended Rhetoric, demographics and control". The Toulminian method successfully analyzed responses.

Future Research Questions: The study used business professional students who wrote the essays to complete an assignment. Most essays generalized Second Life to the broader community of virtual worlds. Future research might apply this methodology to online communities of practice. Can an organization run a community of practice in a virtual world? Would the advantages of the virtual world be worth the additional overhead?

Theme: Virtual Worlds

Reference: Design Principles for Virtual Worlds. (Chaturvedi et al. 2011)

Problem: Virtual Words comprise a new class of information system. What design principles can guide the development of such system?

Importance of the Research: Virtual Worlds are an emerging field and it is difficult to know how to construct them.

Theory Base: Information Systems Design Theory (Updated for virtual worlds.)

Research Approach: Information Systems Design Science Instantiated by "Sentient World" agent based virtual world system.

Outcomes: The authors suggest characteristics of agent-based virtual worlds. The design principles of virtual worlds involve deep structures similar to modeling and simulation designs as well as emergent structures describing unknown user-system knowledge-sharing relationship.

Future Research Questions: How can designers combine analytical, computational, semantic and empirical research methods to appropriately study virtual communities?

Theme: Virtual Worlds

Reference: From Space to Place: Predicting Users' Intentions to Return to Virtual Worlds. (Goel et al.)

Problem: What factors cause consumers to return to virtual worlds?

Importance of the Research: Virtual worlds fail if members do not come back after an initial visit.

Theory Base: The interactionist theory of place attachment.

Research Approach: The authors performed a lab "Quasi-Experiment". Groups of students performed a complex task in Second Life and the responded with their intention to return.

Outcomes: A meaningful experience, or deep involvement, known as a state of cognitive absorption drives the intention to return. When a person loses track of time, they are likely to come back.

Future Research Questions: Future experiments could control aspects of focus, nimbus, etc pr test tasks of varying levels of complexity. How do users' intentions to return change after a longer exposure to he virtual world. Future research might try to control for participants already familiar with 3-D environment

Theme: Virtual worlds

Reference: Co-creation in Virtual Worlds: The Design of the User Experience. (Kohler et al. 2011)

Problem: Virtual worlds that allow the members to create and enhance the experience for other members use co-creation systems. What principles can designers use to create successful co-creation systems?

Importance of the Research: Success of virtual worlds depends largely on the ability of the members to enhance the environment with their own creations

Theory Base: Information Systems Design theory

Research Approach: The authors conducted action and design research and created, implemented, evaluated, and improved their "Ideation Quest" software.

Outcomes: Authors suggest a framework of design guidelines for co-creation systems.

Future Research Questions: Do any of the particular guidelines result in increases in use of the virtual world? How do virtual co-creation compare with other types of co-creation on the web? How does Second Life differ from other virtual communities? Other than idea generation, how can designers create systems to support other co-creation tasks?

Theme: Virtual Worlds

Reference: Enhancing Brand Equity through Flow and Telepresence: A comparison of 2-D and 3D Virtual Worlds. (Nah et al. 2011)

Problem: Do three dimensional virtual worlds affect consumer behavioral intentions more than two dimensional worlds?

Importance of the Research: Important for design of virtual worlds. How can organizations make sure their environment does not detract from the communication of product information.

Theory Base: Flow (Cognitive Absorption), Telepresence (the user forgets they are in a virtual world), and positive emotions. Distraction – Conflict theory (The environment can overpower the product information).

Research Approach: Reference: Author conducted an experimental design where they created similar two dimensional and three dimensional virtual worlds.

Outcomes: Problem: Three dimensional environments have some advantages over two dimensional environments but the three dimensional environment has some drawbacks as well.

Future Research Questions: Future research might use non-students as subjects or subjects who have more virtual world experience. Future research could test to see if results from the first study apply outside of Second Life. Would the three dimensional environment overpower the ability of the members of an online community of practice to interact?

Theme: Virtual Worlds

Reference: Control Over Virtual Worlds by Game Companies: Issues and Recommendations. (Roquilly 2011)

Theory Base: Problem: Research Approach: What is a sustainable model for how gaming companies can control the development of their virtual world.

Importance of the Research: Outcomes: Important for the commercial success of video games

Theory Base: 5Cs Model

Research Approach: Multidisciplinary literature review and review of contracts from virtual worlds.

Outcomes: Virtual worlds currently use copyright, codes, creativity, community and contracts also known as the "5Cs". The authors make recommendations for contract modification.

Future Research Questions: Future research could define a consistent, valid, international, legal framework. Future researchers could trace the evolution of end user license agreements. Future research could examine how crafting differs from co-creation and user-created content.

ReferencesAgarwal, R., Gupta, A.K., and Kraut, R. "The interplay between digital and social networks," *Information Systems Research* (19:3), Sep 2008, pp 243-252.

Alnuaimi, O.A., Robert, L.P., and Maruping, L.M. "Team Size, Dispersion, and Social Loafing in Technology-Supported Teams: A Perspective on the Theory of Moral Disengagement," *Journal of Management Information Systems* (27:1), Sum, pp 203-230.

Animesh, A., Pinsonneault, A., Yang, S.-B., and Oh, W. "An odyssey into virtual worlds: exploring the impacts of technological and spatial environments on intention to purchase virtual products," *MIS Quarterly* (35:3), p 789.

Arazy, O., Nov, O., Patterson, R., and Yeo, L. "Information Quality in Wikipedia: The Effects of Group Composition and Task Conflict," *Journal of Management Information Systems* (27:4), Spr 2011, pp 71-98.

Ardichvili, A., Page, V., and Wentling, T. "Motivation and barriers to participation in virtual knowledge-sharing communities of practice," *Journal of Knowledge Management* (7:1) 2003, pp 64-64-77.

Ba, S. "Establishing online trust through a community responsibility system," *Decision Support Systems* (31:3) 2001, pp 323-323-336.

Bampo, M., Ewing, M.T., Mather, D.R., Stewart, D., and Wallace, M. "The Effects of the Social Structure of Digital Networks on Viral Marketing Performance," *Information Systems Research* (19:3) 2008, pp 273-273-290,392-394.

Bateman, P.J., Gray, P.H., and Butler, B.S. "The Impact of Community Commitment on Participation in Online Communities," *Information Systems Research* (22:4), Dec 2011, pp 841-854.

Becerra-Fernandez, I., Gonzalez, A., and Sabherwal, R. *Knowledge Management: Challenges, Solutions and Technologies* Pearson Prentice Hall, Phoenix, Arizona, 2004.

Berente, N., Hansen, S., Pike, J.C., and Bateman, P.J. "Arguing the value of virtual worlds: patterns of discursive sensemaking of an innovative technology " *MIS Quarterly* (35:3), p 685.

Bergquist, M., and Ljungberg, J. "The power of gifts: organizing social relationships in open source communities," *Information Systems Journal* (11:4), Oct 2001, pp 305-320.

Butler, B.S. "Membership size, communication activity, and sustainability: A resource-based model of online social structures," *Information Systems Research* (12:4), Dec 2001, pp 346-362.

Campbell, J., Fletcher, G., and Greenhill, A. "Conflict and identity shape shifting in an online financial community," *Information Systems Journal* (19:5) 2009, pp 461-461-478.

Chang, H.H., and Chuang, S.S. "Social capital and individual motivations on knowledge sharing: Participant involvement as a moderator," *Information & Management* (48:1), Jan 2010, pp 9-18.

Chaturvedi, A.R., Dolk, D.R., and Drnevich, P.L. "Design principles for virtual worlds," *MIS Quarterly* (35:3) 2011, p 673.

Cheliotis, G. "From open source to open content: Organization, licensing and decision processes in open cultural production," *Decision Support Systems* (47:3), Jun 2009, pp 229-244.

Chen, C.J., and Hung, S.W. "To give or to receive? Factors influencing members' knowledge sharing and community promotion in professional virtual communities," *Information & Management* (47:4), May 2010, pp 226-236.

Cheung, C.M.K., and Lee, M.K.O. "Understanding the sustainability of a virtual community: model development and empirical test," *Journal of Information Science* (35:3), Jun 2009, pp 279-298.

Chiravuri, A., Nazareth, D., and Ramamurthy, K. "Cognitive Conflict and Consensus Generation in Virtual Teams During Knowledge Capture: Comparative Effectiveness of Techniques," *Journal of Management Information Systems* (28:1), Sum 2011, pp 311-350.

Davis, G.B., and Parker, C.A. *Writing the Doctoral Dissertation*, (Second ed.) Barron's Educational Series, Inc., Hauppage, New York, 1997, p. 141.

de Valck, K., van Bruggen, G.H., and Wierenga, B. "Virtual communities: A marketing perspective," *Decision Support Systems* (47:3) 2009, p 185.

DeSanctis, G., Fayard, A.-L., Roach, M., and Lu, J. "Learning in online forums," *European Management Journal* (21:5) 2003, pp 565-565-577.

Dimoka, A. "What does the brain tell us about trust and distrust? Evidence from a functional neuroimaging study," *MIS Quarterly* (34:2) 2010, p 373.

Duan, W., Gu, B., and Whinston, A.B. "Informational cascades and software adoption on the internet: an empirical investigation," *MIS Quarterly* (33:1), Mar 2009, pp 23-48.

Erat, P., Desouza, K.C., and Kurzawa, M. "Business customer communities and knowledge sharing: exploratory study of critical issues," *European Journal of Information Systems* (15:5) 2006, pp 511-511.

Fang, Y.L., and Neufeld, D. "Understanding Sustained Participation in Open Source Software Projects," *Journal of Management Information Systems* (25:4), Spr 2009, pp 9-50.

Forman, C., Ghose, A., and Wiesenfeld, B. "Examining the relationship between reviews and sales: The role of reviewer identity disclosure in electronic markets," *Information Systems Research* (19:3), Sep 2008, pp 291-313.

Forte, A., Larco, V., and Bruckman, A. "Decentralization in Wikipedia Governance," *Journal of Management Information Systems* (26:1), Sum 2009, pp 49-72.

Ganley, D., and Lampe, C. "The ties that bind: Social network principles in online communities," *Decision Support Systems* (47:3) 2009, p 266.

Goel, L., Johnson, N.A., Junglas, I., and Ives, B. "From Space to Place: Predicting Users' Intentions to Return to Virtual Worlds," *MIS Quarterly* (35:3), p 749.

Gray, B. "Informal Learning in an Online Community of Practice," *Journal of Distance Education* (19:1) 2004, pp 20-20-35.

Gray, P.H., Parise, S., and Iyer, B. "Innovation impacts of using social bookmarking systems," *MIS Quarterly* (35:3) 2011, p 629.

Hahn, J., Moon, J.Y., and Zhang, C. "Emergence of New Project Teams from Open Source Software Developer Networks: Impact of Prior Collaboration Ties," *Information Systems Research* (19:3) 2008, pp 369-369-391,393-395.

Hara, N., and Hew, K.F. "Knowledge-sharing in an online community of health-care professionals," *Information Technology & People* (20:3) 2007, pp 235-235-261.

Hinz, O., and Spann, M. "The Impact of Information Diffusion on Bidding Behavior in Secret Reserve Price Auctions," *Information Systems Research* (19:3) 2008a, pp 351-351-368,393-394.

Hinz, O., and Spann, M. "Managing information diffusion in Name-Your-Own-Price auctions," *Decision Support Systems* (49:4), Nov 2008b, pp 474-485.

Ibrahim, M., and Ribbers, P.M. "The impacts of competence-trust and openness-trust on interorganizational systems," *European Journal of Information Systems* (18:3) 2009, pp 223-223-234.

Iriberri, A., and Leroy, G. "A life-cycle perspective on online community success," *ACM Computing Surveys* (41) 2009, pp 11:11--11:29.

Kane, G.C., and Alavi, M. "Casting the Net: A Multimodal Network Perspective on User-System Interactions," *Information Systems Research* (19:3) 2008, pp 253-253-272,392-393.

Kohler, T., Fueller, J., Matzler, K., and Stieger, D. "Co-creation in Virtual Worlds: The Design of the User Experience," *MIS Quarterly* (35:3) 2011, p 773.

Liu, D., Ray, G., and Whinston, A. "The Interaction Between Knowledge Codification and Knowledge-Sharing Networks," (21) 2010, p 892.

Lu, X., Phang, C.W., and Yu, J. "Encouraging Participation in Virtual Communities through Usability and Sociability Development: An Empirical Investigation," *Data Base for Advances in Information Systems* (42:3), Aug 2011, pp 96-114.

Ma, M., and Agarwal, R. "Through a Glass Darkly: Information Technology Design, Identity Verification, and Knowledge Contribution in Online Communities," *Information Systems Research* (18:1) 2007, pp 42-42-67,121-122.

Mayer, A. "Online social networks in economics," *Decision Support Systems* (47:3) 2009, p 169.

Messinger, P.R., Stroulia, E., Lyons, K., Bone, M., Niu, R.H., Smirnov, K., and Perelgut, S. "Virtual worlds - past, present, and future: New directions in social computing," *Decision Support Systems* (47:3) 2009, p 204.

Nah, F.F.-H., Eschenbrenner, B., and DeWester, D. "ENHANCING BRAND EQUITY THROUGH FLOW AND TELEPRESENCE: A COMPARISON OF 2D AND 3D VIRTUAL WORLDS," *MIS Quarterly* (35:3) 2011, p 731.

Phang, C., Kankanhalli, A., and Sabherwal, R. "Usability and Sociability in Online Communities: A Comparative Study of Knowledge Seeking and Contribution*," 2009, p. 721.

Posey, C., Lowry, P.B., Roberts, T.L., and Ellis, T.S. "Proposing the online community self-disclosure model: the case of working professionals in France and the U.K. who use online communities," *European Journal of Information Systems* (19:2) 2010, pp 181-181-195.

Preece, J. "Sociability and usability in online communities: determining and measuring success," *Behaviour & Information Technology* (20:5), Sep-Oct 2001, pp 347-356.

Ransbotham, S., and Kane, G.C. "Membership turnover and collaboration success in online communities: Explaining rises and falls from grace in Wikipedia," *MIS Quarterly* (35:3) 2011, p 613.

Robert, L.P., Dennis, A.R., and Hung, Y.T.C. "Individual Swift Trust and Knowledge-Based Trust in Face-to-Face and Virtual Team Members," *Journal of Management Information Systems* (26:2), Fal 2009, pp 241-279.

Robert, L.P., Jr., Dennis, A.R., and Ahuja, M.K. "Social Capital and Knowledge Integration in Digitally Enabled Teams," *Information Systems Research* (19:3) 2008, pp 314-314-334,392,394.

Romano, N.C., Pick, J.B., and Roztocki, N. "A motivational model for technology-supported cross-organizational and cross-border collaboration," *European Journal of Information Systems* (19:2) 2010, pp 117-117-133.

Roquilly, C. "Control Over Virtual Worlds by Game Companies: Issues and Recommendations.," *MIS Quarterly* (35:3) 2011, p 653.

Sarker, S., Ahuja, M., and Kirkeby, S. "The Role of Communication and Trust in Global Virtual Teams: A Social Network Perspective," *Journal of Management Information Systems* (28:1), Sum 2011, pp 273-309.

Silva, L., Goel, L., and Mousavidin, E. "Exploring the dynamics of blog communities: the case of MetaFilter," *Information Systems Journal*), 2008 2008, pp 1-27.

Suh, A., Shin, K.S., Ahuja, M., and Kim, M.S. "The Influence of Virtuality on Social Networks Within and Across Work Groups: A Multilevel Approach," *Journal of Management Information Systems* (28:1), Sum, pp 351-386.

Thomas, D.M., and Bostrom, R.P. "Vital Signs for Virtual Teams: An Empirically Developed Trigger Model for Technology Adaptation interventions. ," *MIS Quarterly* (34:1) 2010, p 115.

Toral, S.L., Rocio Martinez-Torres, M., Barrero, F., and Cortes, F. "An empirical study of the driving forces behind online communities," *Internet Research* (19:4), 2009 2009, pp 378-392.

Trier, M. "Towards Dynamic Visualization for Understanding Evolution of Digital Communication

Networks," *Information Systems Research* (19:3) 2008, pp 335-335-350,394.

Vaast, E., and Walsham, G. "Trans-Situated Learning: Supporting a Network of Practice with an Information Infrastructure," *Information Systems Research* (20:4) 2009, pp 547-547-564,605-606.

Wareham, J., and Robey, D. "The Role of Online Trading Communities in Managing Internet Auction Fraud," *MIS Quarterly* (31:4) 2007, pp 759-759-781.

Wasko, M.M., Teigland, R., and Faraj, S. "The provision of online public goods: Examining social structure in an electronic network of practice," *Decision Support Systems* (47:3), Jun 2009, pp 254-265.

Xu, B., Jones, D.R., and Shao, B. "Volunteers' involvement in online community based software development," *Information & Management* (46:3) 2009, p 151.